BE A BRILLIANT
BUSINESS WRITER

BE A BRILLIANT
BUSINESS
WRITER

WITHDRAWN

WRITE WELL,
WRITE FAST, and
WHIP the
COMPETITION

Jane Curry and Diana Young

TEN SPEED PRESS
Berkeley

Published in the United States by Celestial Arts, an imprint of the
Crown Publishing Group, a division of Random House, Inc., New York.
www.crownpublishing.com
www.tenspeed.com

Ten Speed Press and the Ten Speed Press colophon are registered
trademarks of Random House, Inc.

The slide on page 146 is used with permission of Michael Alley, *The Craft
of Scientific Presentations*, 2nd ed. (New York: Springer-Verlag, 2010).

Library of Congress Cataloging-in-Publication Data
Curry, Jane (Jane Elizabeth), 1952-
  Be a brilliant business writer : write well, write fast, and whip
the competition /
Jane Curry and Diana Young.
  p. cm.
Includes bibliographical references and index.
1. Business writing. I. Young, Diana, 1956- II. Title.
HF5718.3.C87 2010
651.7′4—dc22
    2010008876

ISBN 978-1-58008-222-8 (alk. paper)

Printed in the United States

Cover and interior text design by Chloe Rawlins

10 9 8 7 6 5 4 3 2 1

First Edition

To my favorite child:
you know who you are.

Contents

Introduction

If a man has nothing to say, he should refrain from giving evidence of that fact in writing.

— GEORGE ELIOT

Succeeding in corporate America is challenging in the best of times, but when economic conditions are weak, demands increase—and fewer people are asked to do more—and in less time. In fact, many of you are so pressed for time you often have to slam away at your keyboards into the night, working against impossible and competing deadlines. No wonder most of you appear to need a good cry, a dry martini, and a long nap.

Like you, people who read business documents are crying, too, and wishing they could drink martinis and take naps, although not with you. Yet, corporate America almost fights against writing efficiency. Look around you: the landscape is littered with lost opportunities buried in the vast pit of empty words that is the final resting place of most business writing.

It's not that business people don't know that good writing is important or can't write; it's that they don't know how to write what counts. So many words are spewed out in the course of every business day like so much toxic waste, and their pernicious effect limits what businesses can accomplish both by eliminating the potential for reflection and discussion and by delaying action.

This book is designed to help you write well, write fast, and whip the competition. This book is for you if you understand that writing is more than a soft skill that everyone already knows how to do. Embrace this book if you see writing as an economic engine that can help you:

- Increase profits
- Influence decisions
- Serve your professional reputation
- Support your firm's strategic goals.

You already know how to write

Since you already know how to write, you don't need or have time to learn a whole new approach to writing: what you need are strategies that can help you leverage your skills so that you can write more effective documents in less time—within the political context of corporate America. You need strategies that can help you elevate your voice above the corporate drone and help you achieve the business results you want.

Forget what you learned in school

If you want to increase your productivity, forget what you learned in school: forget outlining with Roman numerals, forget brainstorming, and stop obsessing about whether you need a comma before "and" in a series. Focus on what counts, on what will improve your readers' understanding and prompt the outcomes you want.

Using this book, you can tap into strategies that will help you achieve the measurable economic benefits of effective writing: more business won, new efficiencies achieved, and more professional satisfaction and security.

Just turn to any page.

CHAPTER 1:

If you want to write persuasively

As you know, persuasive writing is **not** a soft skill—it is economically and professionally central to your success in corporate America. Persuasive writing confers a competitive advantage and allows you to highlight your relevance, which in turn helps you keep your job, strengthen your relationships, and win more business.

If you want to write persuasively, forget about building to your conclusions and sounding like the genius you wish you were. Then, apply the following five principles:

1. **Organize so your key points are clear**
2. **Include only relevant content**
3. **Make sure readers actually read and respond to what you've written (see chapter 2)**
4. **Write clearly and concisely (see chapter 3)**
5. **Write with the right tone (see chapter 4).**

1. Organize so your key points are clear

Organize your content so that your communications deliver the outcomes you want.

Make sure every opening sentence in every email and document passes the "So what?" test

You have no claim on your readers' time, so if there's even a chance readers could respond to the opening sentence of your document or email by saying "So what?" or by asking "And how is this relevant or important to me?" you need to revise the opening so they know exactly why they should keep reading.

Here are a few typical irritatingly useless opening sentences from email; all fail the "So what?" test, and work better than Ambien or narcolepsy at putting readers to sleep.

Opening sentences that fail the "So what?" test

> My name is John Grant, and I work in the marketing department at Branding, Inc.

> I have attached a summary of the analysis we conducted last week of the Gigabyte Gateway.

> Over the past few months the procurement department has been evaluating its vendor relationships as well as the expectations associated with those relationships.

The following sentences pass the "So what?" test, making clear to readers why they should keep reading, especially if they want to be loved.

Opening sentences that pass the "So what?" test

> I work with Anne Bradstreet at Branding, Inc., and am wondering if you have any data on teenage users of your social networking site.

> Please let me know if you have any questions about the attached summary of our analysis of the Gigabyte Gateway.

> We would like to meet with you next week to talk about our relationship in the coming year.

Put your key point first in the topic sentence of every paragraph

Your readers pay attention to the first sentence or two of every paragraph, and then they *drop like flies*. In fact, by the middle of the second sentence, most readers are already thinking about whether they can last another hour without a plate of fries. That's why putting your key points first is critical.

So, never organize academically; in other words, never write to build suspense. We have mystery novels for this.

Original—poor academically organized paragraph with key point misplaced in last sentence

> The team's analysis is enhanced through a continuous and lively dialogue between all team members and management. An important part of the team's role is to communicate their views to the entire management team. Managers play a pivotal role as it is their responsibility to challenge and question analysts' views and assumptions continually. In the end, we believe better client recommendations are made as a result of this rigorous ongoing discussion.

Unlike the poorly organized paragraph above, the following passage begins by highlighting information that's compelling for readers; when you are trying to decide what information should go in the first sentence—in client correspondence in particular—stay away from beginning with details about yourself or your firm; readers will find this as off-putting as people who wear ties identifying them by name (RON).

Instead, make your first sentences serve your clients' or readers' needs by focusing on the value you offer.

Revision—with key point in the topic position

> We provide you with better recommendations as a result of our rigorous review and discussion. To ensure that our decisions are informed by a thoughtful and demanding review:
>
> - Our analysts constantly discuss the results of their research with managers and their teams
> - Our managers are charged with challenging and questioning the analysts' views and assumptions.

In the poorly organized original below, you'll see how overloading your openings with details and failing the "So what?" test will make readers' eyeballs spin like slot machine tumblers in seizure-like displays of frustration.

Original—begins with mind-numbing detail that no one will ever read, including you

> Re: Concern
>
> Dear Tony,
>
> As you asked at our meeting last week, I've completed a multiple regression analysis of the twelve factors that are impeding our ability to address the lack of an efficient way for us to evaluate the ROI generated by our internal training indicatives (as stipulated by policy #2451a, in effect as of 10.09.10). This lack is counterproductive to our Training Goals and fosters mistrust. My analysis was not fruitful and therefore, I would like to make another suggestion about how to get the new Training Assessment done. Since it involves so many divisions and activities, I recommend that we establish a coordinated system between our divisions because doing so would be a good test of our new cooperative environment and help us assess both our abilities and this training initiative.
>
> I'll call you soon to follow up. In the meantime, you can reach me either by email or on my cell phone at 123.456.7890. Thanks.
>
> Lucia

No emotionally healthy person will read past the phrase "multiple regression analysis" unless threatened with a hog-stunner. Think of it this way: if you begin any document with a series of details strung together like cheap plastic beads, you'll cheapen your ideas, and readers will know you shop for meaning at the intellectual equivalent of Wal-Mart.

Let your first sentence shine by immediately making clear why readers need to keep reading.

Revision—email with clear topic sentence and without irrelevant coma-inducing details

Re: Recommendation for addressing assessment of new training initiative

Dear Tony,

I have a solution for addressing the issues raised last week about our new Training Initiative.

I recommend that we establish a coordinated system between our divisions as a test of our new cooperative environment and to help us assess the Training Initiative.

Right now, we have no system to ensure our divisions can work together, which is counterproductive to our training goals and fosters mistrust.

I'll call you soon to follow up. In the meantime, you can reach me either by email or by cell at 123.456.7890. Thanks.

Lucia

When you are done writing, **review your topic sentences and make sure they create an outline of your key points**.

Outline of key points—client letter with a series of good topic sentences

Dear Dr. Thomas,

I am contacting you on behalf of Western University (WU) to request your participation in an *Animal Facilities Benchmark Study.*

WU has hired my firm, Academic Consulting, to conduct a comprehensive assessment of research administration. As part of this assessment, we are working with Dr. Beth Zelano, the Director of WU's Center for Comparative Medicine, to gather data on staffing levels and animal use volume in facilities at peer research institutions.

How you can benefit from participating in this study
We will share all of the data collected with all the institutions that provided the data. In addition to WU, we have also contacted Duke University, Emory University, Stanford University, the University of Illinois at Chicago, the University of Michigan, Washington University, and Yale University.

The information we are seeking
The attached spreadsheet shows the information we are seeking. This data should be relatively easy to compile, particularly the census data, which is similar to what is required for AAALAC accredited institutions. For this study, we have targeted Directors, Assistant Directors, Facility Managers, and Business Managers. If you feel someone else at your institution would be more appropriate to complete the template, please let us know his or her name and email address.

Timeframe
We ask that you please return the completed template by **June 6, 2010.** I will be happy to answer any of your questions; please just call or email me.

Thank you for considering our request.

2. Include only relevant content

To determine what content and details you should include and what you should exclude, you need to distinguish relevant from irrelevant details.

Distinguish relevant from irrelevant details

Relevant details help improve both your readers' understanding and the quality of the decisions they make; irrelevant details make readers want to orchestrate your transfer to the godforsaken settlement of Wayfar on the planet Tatoonine.

So how much detail do your readers need? Not this much:

Original—with tedious, irrelevant details

> Martha,
>
> I know that you are probably not the correct person to contact about this, but I thought you could possibly point me in the right direction. I found a position for one of my friends on the job post page on the intranet and he ended up getting the interview and being hired back in June. I know he put my name down as a referral on the application and he mentioned it in the interview process to his HR contact. We were told in our orientation that if you bring people into the company who get hired you receive a referral bonus after their first six months. Well my friend's six-month anniversary is coming up at the end of November and I was looking to find the correct contact to make sure I would be receiving the bonus and around when it could be expected. I would greatly appreciate any advice you could give me. Thanks.

Will Martha live long enough to care about the writer's endless, narcissistic detail? No. Now read the revision that follows.

Revision—with only relevant details

Martha,

Do you know who in HR handles referral bonuses? If you are not the right person to contact, can you point me in the right direction? I would love to collect my bonus!

Thanks for your help.

Now, consider the next example from an industry analysis, which calls to mind Isaiah 6:11: "Then said I, Lord, how long?" All the writer needed to do in this document was explain the kinds of coal the company mines.

Original—a slag heap of meaningless detail

Coal Overview

Coal is classified as a fossil fuel. It is an organic, combustible sedimentary rock derived from vegetation that accumulated under conditions that prevented complete decay. Coal is generally classified into five major categories based on the amount of transformation undergone from the earlier plant and peat stages, heating value, and other characteristics:

1. Peat: consists of partly decomposed vegetation remains, has a high oxygen and water content and represents the first stage in the coalification process.

2. Brown coal or lignite: a brownish-black coal with generally high moisture and ash content, and the lowest carbon content and heating value. These coals have a relatively low carbon content, about 60% to 75% on a dry basis and high moisture content, ranging between 30% and 70%. These coals are difficult to transport due to a susceptibility of spontaneous combustion. Lignite has an average heat content of 13 million Btu per short ton with an ignition temperature of approximately 600°F.

3. Sub-bituminous: a dull, black coal with a higher heating value than brown coals and lignite. Carbon contents are higher than brown coals, ranging from 71% to 77% with mois-

ture content of about 20%. Sub-bituminous coal has an average heat content of 18 million Btu per short ton.

4. Bituminous: a soft, intermediate grade of coal that is the most common and widely used in the United States. Carbon content ranges from 78% to 91% with water content of 1.5% to 7%. Bituminous coal has an average heat content of 24 million Btu per short ton with an ignition temperature of approximately 800°F.

5. Anthracite: the hardest type of coal, consisting of nearly pure carbon. Anthracite has the highest heating value and the lowest moisture and ash content. It typically has carbon content greater than 92% and very low moisture content. It is difficult to ignite but has a high heating value. Anthracite has an average heat content of 25 million Btu per short ton with an ignition temperature of approximately 950°F.

Furthermore, coal can have two additional classifications: (1) Steam, also called thermal, and (2) Metallurgical, also called coking. The most significant distinguishing characteristic is whether or not the coal is agglomerating (to make into or become an untidy mass). Of the five ranks listed above, bituminous is commonly agglomerating and, hence, all bituminous coals are coking coals, but not all have the other necessary characteristics (low sulfur, etc.) to make them metallurgical. This does not preclude these coals from being used as steam coal and, in fact, a vast majority is consumed as steam coal. The basic requirements for a coking coal to have the designation of a metallurgical coal are: volatile matter up to 35%; low sulfur content (less than 1.25%); and a reasonably low, but uniform ash content (ash content of less than 8%). These general requirements have become even less specific over the years as coke producers, especially the Japanese, have greatly improved their techniques for blending metallurgical coals to produce very high-quality coke.

Such overstuffed writing demands that your readers have the cognitive stamina to keep scrolling down until they finally unearth something meaningful. Most readers don't—and they won't be convinced of your intelligence by having to sift through endless detail. Notice how the following revision spares readers frustration and saves them time.

Revision—with only meaningful detail

Coal Overview

Baron Co. mines two kinds of coal:

1. Steam: also called thermal, which is quite common.

2. Metallurgical: also called coking, which comes from bituminous coal. Coke producers, however, especially the Japanese, have greatly improved their techniques for blending metallurgical coals to produce very high-quality coke.

As we often say to our husbands, "Just because you know something doesn't make it useful or interesting to anyone else." Same goes for your readers.

Identify the specific benefits clients will receive

Distinguish yourself from your competition and sharpen your competitive advantage by showing clients how they'll benefit, thanks to you and your firm. In other words, be sure to:

- **Identify the benefits and added value** of your ideas, your products, and your services, instead of just highlighting their features.

- **Reassure clients you understand their needs and challenges**—whether time constraints, budget issues, complex economic challenges, or whatever.

- **Avoid sending out client letters or emails that are so general** you could send them to *any* client, with only a name change; you'll recognize these communications because the topics discussed could potentially apply to the entire universe of customers, both known and unknown.

- **Present your firm's qualifications without pretense.** Your readers are not really interested in how big your firm is, how many awards your CEO has received, or how many collective years of experience you have. Your clients are interested in how you can help them achieve their goals.

Instead of focusing on the customer's needs and offering solutions, the next example focuses on how wonderful Community Bank is and sounds like a form letter that could be sent to *any* customer.

Original—weak, generic customer letter

Dear Mr. Mather:

Thank you for the opportunity to submit this proposal for your banking relationship.

Community Bank, a wholly owned subsidiary of Banner Bankcorp, Inc., is a $700 million community bank, serving customers throughout Macomb County and the surrounding communities. We are part of one of the largest networks of community banks in the Macomb area, delivering financial products and services to one of every five households in the Macomb area through 180 locations.

Community Bank would welcome the opportunity to develop a long-term relationship with Research Inc. This proposal and pricing information serves as an example of our interest and desire to do business with Research Inc. Our approach is to proactively work with our clients to help them find solutions to their banking needs. We enlist the expertise of our Community associates as part of the relationship and make recommendations to improve on the services that clients are currently receiving at this time.

This proposal summarizes a term loan and a revolving line of credit. In addition, other bank products and services are discussed.

Very truly yours,

T. Tomlins

Now consider the revised customer letter that identifies the client-specific benefits of doing business with Community Bank, and focuses more on the customer and less on the bank.

*Revision—letter that highlights specific client needs
and solutions*

Dear Mr. Mather,

We are pleased to submit the following proposal for our banking relationship with you. We want your business, and we are committed to doing all we can to exceed your expectations by providing products and services that will help you achieve your goals.

We have customized our recommendations based on your objectives, and are confident we can:

- **Provide you with the funds you need** to meet your growth objectives over the next two years
- **Give you faster access to your funds** through our specialized cash management services
- **Reduce the interest expense** you now incur.

You can count on us to put our extensive resources to work to help you find the best possible solutions to your banking needs. To that end, we will enlist the expertise of our experienced Community Bank team, who will help you improve the services you now receive and help you meet tomorrow's challenges.

I look forward to talking with you about the enclosed proposal and pricing information, which summarizes a term loan, a revolving line of credit, and other bank products and services designed to help your business succeed.

Next steps
I will call you on Monday to follow up. In the meantime, you can always reach me at 312.000.0000.

Again, thank you for your interest in doing business with us.

Sincerely yours,

T. Tomlins

So put your readers first—put first what will serve their needs, and leave out what you know, but they don't need.

CHAPTER 2:

If you want readers to actually read and respond to what you've written

Your readers don't have time to read everything they should read—and neither do you. In fact, in this age of information overload, unrelenting details, and endless distractions, most readers don't even have time to tie their shoes or brush their teeth—so never forget the biggest secret of business writing:

Nobody actually wants to read what you have written.

Jeremy Silverman, Managing Director at Frontenac, a private investment firm in Chicago, says, "In our business, time is our most precious resource... If our investment professionals have to hunt for key facts in a memo, or struggle to follow the writer's logic, time is wasted and efficiency dies. Good writing is more than a "nice-to-have" skill—like playing the cello or having a great outside jump shot—good writing is an essential driver of our productivity."

Can you increase productivity for your readers? Can you help them access your key messages at the speed of light, or at least before the dawn of a new age? Yes, you can—if you make your message instantly visible by using visual tools—and if you remember that most readers **devote only about 4.5 seconds** to any given email, letter, or memo.

This section identifies five strategies that will help you increase the persuasive impact of your writing **by making your message clear at a glance:**

1. **Use informative Re: lines**

2. **Use headings and subheadings to make your logic and judgments clear at a glance**

3. **Use typeface variety to emphasize key points**

4. **Use bullets and numbering to highlight important information**

5. **Use graphs, tables, and charts to share complex financial and technical data.**

These tools apply no matter what you are writing—an email, a letter, a transaction analysis—and no matter who your target audience is.

If your manager loves long paragraphs and won't let you use bullets and boldface, here are your options:

- **Solicit your manager's buy-in before you use formatting in your documents.** Offer examples from this book, and explain how making the message clear increases persuasive impact and strengthens relationships with readers.

- **Start looking for a new position.** If you can't get your manager's buy-in, he or she is a stylistic Neanderthal. Just know that you are far more evolved, and therefore, a far superior being.

1. Use informative Re: lines

Think of your Re: line as the global heading on the map of the page, which imparts important information. The most common mistake is a Re: line that doesn't tell you enough about the message—either because it's overly general or overly specific.

Ineffective Re: lines don't give enough information

Re: Vacation

Re: Briefing

Re: Survey

Re: LC32456

*Effective Re: lines are informative and
give readers the goods at a glance*

Re: Emergency vacation starting tomorrow

Re: Friday 8 a.m. briefing for all analysts with Mr. Marks

Re: Please return Product Opinion Survey by Friday, April 13

Re: Update on resolved problems with account LC32456

2. Use headings and subheadings to make your logic and judgments clear at a glance

Most of you are probably already using headings in some of your documents to help your readers:

- **See your key ideas** without effort so they don't miss anything important

- **Find what interests them**, since no one is interested in everything you have to say and no one has time to read everything he or she should read

- **Gain some control** over where they spend their time. For this act of kindness alone, readers will speak of you in hushed and reverential tones.

We encourage you to consider using headings and subheadings in *everything* you write—whether short or long.

In the example below, readers are too distracted by the sizzling sound of their own brains frying to extricate any meaningful information—despite the glorious and imagined hint of garlic.

Original—email without headings to guide readers

Bob,

The teams currently performing installations have had serious and ongoing problems because they must troubleshoot products outside their scope and they can't provide the quality of service because they don't have the necessary product understanding. This is a difficult situation when the teams are performing installations in front of customers and they apparently don't know what they are doing. I think that we need a list of products and the teams that have the operational knowledge to install these products. Another thing that would be good would be if we could have some product installation manuals that teams could take with them, so if they have to install an unfamiliar product they have the information they need. Therefore, could you let me know what your thinking on this is? Please advise.

If you're not using subheadings to give your readers instant access to your message, you decrease the chances that anyone will respond. This revision makes a prompt response at least possible:

Revision—with headings to guide readers

Bob,

We need your help!

What we need to improve product installations
We need a list of products, the teams that know how to install these products, and product installation manuals.

Background on problem
The teams performing installations must troubleshoot products outside their scope, and they can't provide quality service

because they don't have the necessary product understanding. This does not inspire customer confidence.

Next steps
I will call you in the next few days so we can set up a meeting with the team leaders to discuss this recommendation. If you have any questions or need more information, please call me at my summer home on the coast of France.

Formatting can be an issue when you are writing to someone whose PC doesn't share the same platform. If you are not sure if your formatting will translate on the other end, you'll have to format your document manually. You can type in dashes for bullets, use numbers for numbered lists, and use capital letters when you write headings and subheadings.

Use subheadings in longer documents

When you write longer documents that already have standard main headings, use subheadings within these established sections to make your reports even easier to navigate. Subheadings help you identify key categories of information, making complex information easier to understand, and therefore, more persuasive.

Pour yourself a stiff drink and then scan the example on page 18.

Lies your teachers told you: "A paragraph is always five sentences long: an introduction, a three-sentence body, and a conclusion." This would be correct if your paper is titled something like "Our Friend the Beaver" and you are in elementary school—but you're not. Today you're writing client letters and emails in which a paragraph might be a single line long, as in "Thanks for making time for lunch last week." If you're writing anything else—credit analyses, procedures, white papers, reports of any kind—your paragraph length is determined by the content. If you only have three sentences worth of information, your paragraph is three sentences long. And there are no page requirements anymore, either!

Company Overview

Better Health, LLC ("Better Health" or the "Company"), which is headquartered in Ravine, Idaho, is a leading health plan management company serving self-insured organizations throughout the Billings, Montana metropolitan region. Currently, Better Health's customer base is comprised almost exclusively of self-insured labor unions. The Company has developed a proprietary preferred provider network ("PPO") that is comprised of over 66,000 physicians, hospitals, and diagnostic specialists located primarily in Montana and Wyoming, making it one of the largest PPOs in the greater Billings, Montana area. In addition to granting network access, Better Health also offers its PPO customers a broad range of third party administrative ("TPA") services, such as claims repricing and adjudication, as well as other value-added services such as eligibility management, beneficiary enrollment, medical management services and ongoing customer service to help them better manage their total health care costs. Currently, the Company provides services to over 156,000 employees and over 445,000 members, making it one of the largest independent health plan management companies in the Idaho region. In addition, as a result of the Company's acquisition of Rural Ramblings during 2006, employees served will increase to at least 176,000, with total members served of over 500,000 by the end of the first quarter of 2007. Since December 2002, the Company has been owned by Farmer Partners ("FP" or the "Sponsor"). For the TTM period ended October 31, 2009, Better Health generated revenue and EBITDA of $43.2 million and $17.6 million, respectively, with fiscal year end 2009 revenue and EBITDA expected to be $43.6MM and $18.4MM, respectively.

You can see why the original necessitates straight whiskey. Save your readers from the inevitable path to a 12-step program by making it easier for them to navigate your message.

*Revision—with headings to break up long paragraphs
and make meaning clear*

Company Overview

Headquartered in Ravine, Idaho, Better Health, LLC ("BH," the "Company") is one of the largest health plan management companies serving self-insured organizations in the Billings, Montana area. After acquiring Rural Ramblings in 2006, will increase from 156,000 employees served to at least 176,000, with total members served increasing from 400,000 to over 500,000 by the end of the first quarter of 2007. Better Health's customer base is comprised almost exclusively of self-insured labor unions. Since December 2002, the Company has been owned by Farmer Partners ("FP," or the "Sponsor").

Revenues

For the TTM period ended October 31, 2009, BH generated revenue and EBITDA of $43.2 million and $17.6 million, respectively, with FYE 2009 revenue and EBITDA expected to be $43.6MM and $18.4MM, respectively.

Product Offerings

The Company provides a proprietary preferred provider network ("PPO") comprised of over 66,000 physicians, hospitals, and diagnostic specialists in Montana and Wyoming, making it one of the largest PPOs in the greater Billings area.

In addition, the firm offers a broad range of third party administrative ("TPA") services, such as claims repricing and adjudication, and other value-added services such as eligibility management, beneficiary enrollment, medical management services, and ongoing customer service.

Headings and subheadings are especially important when you have to send an email or a document to a **diverse group of readers**, who may have different needs. Headings and subheadings give these various readers access to the information that interests them most, and doesn't force them to wade through rivers of details they don't care about.

Thanks to the headings, the following email will meet the needs of:

- **Senior managers**, who want to know only about the recommendation and the request
- **Support personnel**, who need to read the background information, too.

Example—using headings to meet the diverse needs of a diverse audience

At your request, I have developed the following recommendations for your approval; these recommendations are designed to help Coverage Capital improve its performance, and help us increase our overall customer satisfaction levels and operational capacity.

Recommendation
To achieve these goals, I recommend that we assign an internal review team to help identify Coverage Capital's performance issues and share best practices. We know from prior experience that such teams can help our divisions improve.

Request
If you agree with my recommendations, please let me know, and I'll assign the review team and schedule the next steps.

Background on issue
Coverage Capital's performance levels continue to remain below standards, even though its performance is becoming an increasingly important issue as claim volumes continue their annual double-digit increases.

Use headings and subheadings in announcements and updates

Most readers are trying to figure out where they're going **when they are already ten minutes late and running for the elevator**. Don't make their lives harder by burying the crucial information in the middle of a killer paragraph. Instead, use bolded subheadings along with indented block in updates and meeting announcements; this will catch your reader's eye in a hurry.

Announcement so clear you can read it on your Blackberry while swimming laps

> **What:** The Next Endless Staff Improvement Meeting
>
> **When:** Thursday, December 24, 2010, 4:00 p.m. - ??
>
> **Where**: Tiny Hot Conference Room A

3. Use typeface variety to emphasize key points

Use different typefaces, such as **bold** and ***bold italics***, to highlight key information you don't want readers to miss, so you get the response you need. Avoid using underlining—the tired or careless eye easily confuses underlined text with website addresses.

Example—using boldface judiciously so readers see what you need and can respond quickly

> Tarzan,
>
> Could you review the attached synopses for publication in the next issue of *The Primate Quarterly*?
>
> Sheena of the Jungle told me you might have time. Will you let me know **if you can get me your feedback by Wednesday, September 24**?
>
> Thanks,
>
> Kamala the Wolf Girl

Just assume that your readers are in the same situation you are: overworked, underpaid, and constantly in need of more praise. If you acknowledge that reality, you will use tools like boldface and bullets to alleviate their suffering.

Example—using boldface to highlight key information

> Fraser,
>
> This latest draft reflects input from Kathryn, Anne, David, Bill, and me. Since many of the same people will be at Jim's meeting tomorrow, this working draft will help focus our discussion and refine the piece. The attached describes:
>
> - **The key issues** we are facing
> - **Our recommended approach to addressing these issues**
> - **A framework for assessing the right solution**, based on client objectives and constraints.
>
> Thanks—looking forward to our meeting tomorrow.

A word to the wise

Please don't ever use Ariel Narrow 9-point font, as this is the font of blind despair and premature aging. In fact, if you *ever* use this font, you will be transported to the remote planet Hoth, which is covered in snow and ice and frequently pelted by meteorites.

If your firm has a standard font, go with that. If not, use:

- **Times New Roman** (12)
- **Ariel** (10 or 11)
- **Verdana** (9 or 10)
- **Garamond** (12)

Capital punishment

Since you are already reading this book, we are confident you aren't using all caps to hurl a screaming wall of words at readers because you know that doing so reduces everything to the same level of inane emphasis. However, if you have associates who are doing so, leave this page open on their desks.

USE ALL CAPS ONLY WHEN YOU WANT YOUR READERS TO FEEL AS THOUGH YOU ARE YELLING AT THEM.

USE ALL BOLD CAPS ONLY IF YOU WANT YOUR READERS TO REGRET THE DAY YOU WERE BORN.

<u>USE ALL BOLD UNDERLINED CAPS ONLY WHEN YOU WANT TO BE TAKEN TO AN UNDISCLOSED LOCATION, WHERE SOME JOHN-ASHCROFT-LIKE BEING WILL HELP YOU OUT—OR NOT.</u>

There's one exception to this rule, and that's when you're addressing life-threatening issues. For example, we once taught some very important scientists who were intelligent enough to send around this email in all bold caps:

PLEASE DO NOT STORE RADIOACTIVE LEAD BRICKS IN THE COMMON LIVING AREAS.

If you're dealing with dangerous levels of radioactivity in the office, feel free to bring out the big guns.

4. Use bullets and numbering to highlight important information

Using bullets and numbering:

- Helps your readers process and respond to your message in less time
- Shows your readers respect by acknowledging that they don't have time to read through long paragraphs
- Increases the value readers assign to you and your communications because they'll never miss critical actions, insights, judgments, benefits, or outcomes
- Spares you from wasting precious time writing explanatory follow-up emails and taking time-sucking phone calls.

In particular, bullets and numbering allow you to break up unreadably long paragraphs. Such long paragraphs diminish the chance readers will actually read what you've written unless they have a form of OCD that requires them to read every single word.

Try to read the following paragraph, straight from a standard consulting report.

Original—paragraph from the depths where even the fish are blind (233 words)

> All emails should be stored and retrieved in the original format allowing a user to retrieve or access a copy of the intended record back to their active mail file at a future date. All normal actions should be performed on the email and disposition rules must be associated with that copy. Internal transmissions of emails that have been declared as company records must be marked as "Copy of Company Record" (or similar notation) in the recipient's email. Recipients must be able to delete, store temporarily, or capture as a new record any Copy of Company Record that they receive. They cannot modify a Copy of Company Record without creating a new email document. It is important that external recipients have no knowledge of the records status and that the email classifications of company records are visible to internal recipients. To support the client's existing email environment, the classification process must be consistent, whether a user is working with the Outlook, client, or web access. It must support Exchange XXI and the management capabilities beyond email messages and their attachments, i.e., calendar entries (and attached documents), contacts, notes, and journals.

Now, imagine that you have to summarize this paragraph *without* a second reading or you have to die. Will you live? Not likely.

Revision—using bullets and boldface (182 words)

The system must:

- **Store all emails** in the original format so users can retrieve or access copies and perform normal actions on the email, including disposal.

- **Identify emails declared as company records** with Copy of Company Record in the recipient's email. The system must also have a consistent classification process, whether a user is working with Outlook, the client, or web access.

- **Allow internal recipients** to:

  - Delete, store, or capture all Copy of Company Records; a Copy of Company Record cannot be copied without creating a new email document.

  - See the email classifications of company records.

- **Ensure that external recipients** have no knowledge of the record status.

- **Support Exchange XXI** and the management capabilities beyond email messages and their attachments, such as calendar entries (and attached documents), contacts, notes, and journals.

When to use numbers instead of bullets

In general, use numbering to indicate priority, to indicate sequence, to explain instructions, or to match a specific number of points to an introductory sentence or phrase, as in *The company faces four significant challenges.*

The single paragraph on page 26 from a longer document full of dense paragraphs left readers wailing as if at the gates of Hell itself.

Original—long paragraph that repels readers

It should also be noted that NVA, and other industry consolidators, have a significant competitive advantage as they benefit from economies of scale in training alienologists on new techniques and purchasing new equipment for multiple hospitals in multiple galaxies. This trend in improved training and upgraded equipment has occurred over the last decade or so. Finally, cash is paid at the time of service for approximately 98% of revenue, negating any collection issues typical of human health care. As courts consider aliens personal property, minimal malpractice risk exists in the companion alien care market.

Now, see how numbering helps excavate the supporting details, reduce reading time, and make the message clear at a glance?

Revision—with numbers that pull out supporting details and pull in readers

NVA enjoys three advantages over smaller alien healthcare operations:

1. **Economies of scale in training and equipment costs.** NVA can train alienologists for less and purchase equipment for less because it operates in multiple hospitals in multiple galaxies.

2. **Minimal collection issues.** Cash is paid at the time of service for 98% of revenue.

3. **Minimal malpractice risk** as aliens are considered property.

Using numbers or bullets is also helpful because these tools create a checklist of actions for readers to follow. If you're asking your readers to do something, every bullet will probably start with a verb. See how long it takes you to locate the relevant actions hidden in this next chunk of text.

August 6, 1970

Dear Mr. Madoff,

As we discussed, please sign the two enclosed documents to indicate you turned over your life to us at The Bottomless Pit, Inc. The red "sign here" tabs indicate where we need your signature. In addition, you will need to have St. Peter sign the certificate of abandonment, which means you no longer work for the Rapture Corporation; you work for us. Please also be sure to fill in the appropriate dates on the two documents. You can then return these completed documents to me in the envelope I've provided for your convenience.

We look forward to working with you!

All the best,

Lucifer
Prince of Darkness

Most people don't have the time to read such dense instructions—especially when they're busy setting up global Ponzi schemes. Instead, save yourself and your readers aggravation by using verbs to list the actions they must take to meet your endless, petty demands. (Who's surprised that hell requires a lot of forms?)

*Revision—with numbering to help the reader see
the steps he must take with less effort*

August 6, 1970

Dear Mr. Madoff,

As we discussed, please:

1. **Sign the two enclosed documents** to indicate you signed over your life to us as a new employee of The Bottomless Pit, Inc. The red "sign here" tabs indicate where you need to sign.

2. **Have St. Peter sign the certificate of abandonment**, which means you no longer work for Rapture Corporation; you work for us.

3. **Fill in the appropriate dates** on the two documents.

4. **Return these completed documents to me** in the envelope provided for your convenience.

We look forward to working with you!

All the best,

Lucifer
Prince of Darkness

Make sure all your points are bullet-worthy

Not all points deserve the same emphasis, so use good judgment about when to use bullets or numbering by asking: "Do I want to emphasize these points visually?"

Avoid using bullets or numbering to mark every point

Instead, use introductory phrases or sentences to lead into bulleted and numbered lists or to clarify the relationship among the points you've listed. Don't bullet introductory phrases or sentences because they're not part of the list.

Original—ineffective overuse of bullets with no introductory phrase

- The Clinical Research Department (CRD) conducts and manages clinical research at Nip & Tuck

- A key part of that function will be to simplify the administrative processes supporting research and to actively assist researchers with those processes

- Part of the department's role is to help ensure the protection of Nip & Tuck's patients, personnel, resources, and reputation.

Overusing bullets to mark every point doesn't help organize the information for readers, and will remind those from rural Pennsylvania of deer peppered with buckshot.

Use an introductory phrase to carry the big idea and then bullets to pull out the points. See how the next example's introductory phrase, "The department," begins the sentence that each bullet finishes? This structure works like magic to improve flow and help readers easily understand your logic.

Revision—with a phrase that introduces the bullets

Goals

The Clinical Research Department (CRD) helps conduct and manage clinical research at Nip & Tuck. The department:

- Simplifies the administrative processes supporting research

- Helps researchers with those processes

- Helps protect Nip & Tuck's patients, personnel, resources, and reputation.

Differentiate main from sub-bullets by using different bullet point markers. If you use the same mark for both main and sub-bullets, your readers will have trouble distinguishing your main points from your supporting points, and may become distracted by an urgent impulse to check out televisionwithoutpity.com.

Use parallel structure

Parallel structure means that the first word in each bulleted or numbered point is the same kind of word, or has the same ending as all the other first words in a set of bulleted or numbered points.

Parallel structure:

- **Makes writing flow more smoothly** so it's easier for readers to follow
- **Helps readers see the relationships between your ideas**
- **Assures readers you are not careless** or unschooled, or both.

In the next example, you'll see that each bullet starts with a different kind of word, and lacks parallel structure.

Original—bulleted list without the benefit of parallel structure

Budgetary Goals

We are planning to:

- Continue to structure contracts that enable us to bill the client in advance of incurring costs. Currently, we bill a majority of our clients 50% to 75% up front.
- Management of payables and receivables using current processes will continue.
- It is essential to monitor WIP balances, ensuring we bill and recognize costs in a timely manner.

In the following example, each bullet begins with the same kind of word: a verb with the same ending—continue, manage, and monitor.

Revision—uses parallel structure with actions

Budgetary Goals

We are planning to:

- Continue to structure contracts that enable us to bill clients before incurring costs. Currently, we bill most of our clients 50% to 75% up front.
- Manage payables and receivables using current processes.
- Monitor WIP balances to ensure we bill and recognize costs promptly.

You can also make a parallel list that begins with nouns. Happily, working with nouns requires very little effort, since nouns are all things, and so are already parallel, which means you don't have to worry about their endings. If there is an adjective before the noun, no worries. These descriptive words do not disrupt parallel structure.

Example—parallel structure using nouns

Donald Deco, Inc., one of the leading plastics manufacturing companies in the U.S., has three divisions:

1. The Extrusion Division, which manufactures custom extrusion plastic sheet materials

2. The Color Division, which develops color concentrates for plastic applications

3. The Molded Division, which engineers rotational molded plastic products.

Using bullets to edit out repetition

You'll know you have found a good place to use bullets if you're repeating the same subject at the start of most of your sentences. Used correctly, bullets eliminate repetition and empty words and help you write more concisely.

The following example scores high on the Irritating Index, as it keeps repeating the subject in every bullet.

Original—with irritatingly repetitive subject at the beginning of each bullet (166 words)

- Management indicated that the company's 0.18 micron silicon results in industry-leading read-rates

- The company also indicated that its PICA manufacturing process is scheduled to be operational sometime between March and May

- The company announced a new multiprotocol reader that can read Class 0 and Class 1 products.

If a word or phrase actually applies to every bullet, use it once in the introduction. This strategy will both edit out useless repetition and stop annoying your readers.

Revision—refining bullets to eliminate repetition (139 words)

Management:

- Indicated that the company's 0.18 micron silicon has industry-leading read-rates
- Indicated that its PICA manufacturing process will be operational sometime between March and May
- Announced a new multiprotocol reader that can read Class 0 and Class 1 products.

Use consistent punctuation after bulleted and numbered points

There are several schools of thought about how to capitalize and punctuate bulleted and numbered lists. We don't care which school you adopt as long as you agree with us, so: .

Lies your teacher told you: "Never use bullets/charts/boldface/ subheadings in a letter." In ancient times, corporations sent out dense, bureaucratic letters. Nowadays, customers won't put up with that kind of communication; instead, they'll take their business down the street to the conveniently located, and less loquacious, competition. Rather than writing for your teacher's approval, you're writing to win your readers' understanding, and if you write using large, dense paragraphs, readers will think you're a blockhead, and they may be right.

- **Be consistent:** You can put a period after each sentence, put a period only at the end of the last line, or use no punctuation at the end of each bulleted or numbered point. For capitalization, either stick with all small letters at the start of each point or stick with capitalizing the first word.

- **Do not use commas or semicolons after each bulleted point.** These punctuation marks clutter the page.

- **Find out what your manager prefers—and you prefer it, too.** Some corporations have standard punctuation and capitalization rules, so it's a good idea to know and follow those rules.

5. Use graphs, tables, and charts to share complex financial or technical data

When you have a lot of technical or highly detailed information to share, a table, chart, or diagram can help your readers see and compare the details without resorting to drugs.

To make the best use of charts, graphs, and tables, **introduce your table or chart with an overall statement that clarifies what the details in the table or chart suggest, or what significant trends are displayed.** Your readers should not be asked to *interpret* numbers or technical data. That's your job.

The following paragraph is stuffed with data, and starts with detail, which is never a good beginning.

Original—data-filled paragraph

> Total domestic equities were $153.3 million, or 44% of total assets; total fixed income was $130.9 million, or 38%; total international equities were $38.3 million, or 11%; and total mortgages were $24.2 million, or 7%. The asset allocation meets current guidelines.

The chart that follows allows readers to compare the numbers at a glance—and begins with a topic sentence that provides the overall assessment.

Revision—makes key details accessible in a chart

The asset allocation meets our current guidelines:

Asset	Allocation	Percentage of total assets
Total domestic equities	$153.3 million	44%
Total fixed income	$130.9 million	38%
Total international equities	$38.3 million	11%
Total mortgages	$24.2 million	7%

Even if you don't have lots of numbers to convey, charts can be a source of deep comfort to harried readers. In fact, you can even use charts when you don't have any numbers or technical data to share. Consider the following example.

Original—Night-of-the-Living-Dead paragraph

Nature Lovers Inc. is an international recreational products company focused on the design, manufacture, and marketing of fishing, marine, diving, and camping equipment. In each of the areas in which it competes, Nature Lovers manufactures products with strong brand names. In the fishing/marine division, leading products include Go Fast electric motors, as well as SusieQ and Big SusieQ rods and reels and Reel'em In fishing line. Diving equipment includes the popular Scubaduba line of buoyancy compensators, regulators, and tanks, as well as Jacques Cousteau diving gauges and computers. Finally, camping equipment includes the recognized Cuddle Up, Hot Hiking, and WaterTight lines of tents, backpacks, and accessories in addition to the New Town and Pond Floater canoe and kayak manufacturers.

This original is flailing about in an effort to describe the relationships between divisions and brands, but a chart makes those relationships easily visible. In business writing, sometimes a picture *is* worth a thousand words.

Revision—Sweet-Dawn-of-Love table

Nature Lovers Inc. is an international recreational products company that designs, manufactures, and markets fishing, marine, diving, and camping equipment. In each of the areas in which it competes, Nature Lovers manufactures products with strong brand names:

DIVISION	BRAND—PRODUCTS
Fishing and marine	**Go Fast:** electric motors **SusieQ and Big SusieQ:** rods and reels **Reel'em In:** fishing line
Diving	**Scubaduba:** buoyancy compensators, regulators, tanks **Jacques Cousteau:** diving gauges and computers
Camping	**Cuddle Up, Hot Hiking,** and **WaterTight:** tents, backpacks, accessories **New Town:** canoes, kayaks **Pond Floaters:** canoes, kayaks

Sometimes a table is a better option than using bullets, especially if you want readers to compare numbers.

Original—repetition and excessive bullet use that makes comparing numbers difficult (202 words)

2010 Estimate Changes
- *We are estimating* 2010 revenue of $1.43 billion, which represents 6.3% growth over our 2009 revenue estimate.
- *We are estimating* 2010 gross margin of 64.2%, which is slightly lower than our 2009 estimate. Excluding the $10 million benefit from historic royalties and legal

settlements in 2009, our 2010E gross margin of 64.2% represents 40 bps of expansion.

- *We estimate* 2010 gross margin for CellSong will be about 69.4%, which represents 20 bps of margin compression over our 2009 estimates (20 bps of expansion excluding benefit of historic royalties and legal settlement in 2009).

- *We are estimating* 2010 gross margin for CellAll Systems will be about 52.1%, which represents 100 bps of margin expansion over our 2009 estimates.

- *We are forecasting* 2010 operating margin of 25.4.%, which represents 70 bp of margin expansion over our 2009 estimate. Further, it is our belief that IVGN will leverage its operating expenses and build on its gross margin expansion to deliver EPS growth in the high single digits.

- *We are estimating* 2010 pro forma EPS (including FAS 123R) of $4.80. If the impact of FAS 123R is excluded, our 2010 pro forma EPS estimate is $5.35.

The chart on the opposite page allows readers to easily measure the gap between the 2010 and 2009 estimates. Using charts also automatically edits out the annoying repetition that suggests you are suffering from pre-senile dementia.

Revision—using a table so readers can compare numbers instantly (67 words)

Introducing 2010 Estimates

	2010 estimates	Growth over 2009 estimates	Comments
Revenue	$1.43b	6.3%	
Gross margin	64.2%	40bp	Excluding the $10 million benefit from historic royalties and legal settlements in 2008
Gross margin by CellSong	69.4%	20bp	
Gross margin by CellAll Systems	52.1%	100bp	
Operating margin	25.4%	70bp	Expect IVGN to leverage its operating expenses to deliver low double-digit EPS growth
Pro forma EPS (including FAS 123R)	$4.80		$5.35 excluding FAS 123R

So, welcome to scanning. Remember, nobody "reads" anything anymore: they simply scan and skim, so use formatting to make your meaning inescapably clear.

CHAPTER 3

If you want to write clearly and concisely

Such preparations shall be made as will completely obscure all Federal and nonFederal buildings occupied by the Federal Government during an air raid for any period of time from visibility by reason of internal or external illumination. Such obscuration may be obtained either by black out construction or by termination of the illumination.

—NAMELESS, LONG DEAD AIDE TO PRESIDENT
   FRANKLIN DELANO ROOSEVELT

Tell them that in buildings where they have to keep the work going to put something over the windows; and in buildings where they can let the work stop for a while, to turn out the lights.

—PRESIDENT FRANKLIN DELANO ROOSEVELT'S REVISION

Because you are not a sociopath and don't want to inflict pain on your readers, you want to write clearly and concisely. Unfortunately, the world conspires against such aspirations, creating misconceptions about what makes for effective writing. Think back to college, where long sentences and big words were synonymous with intelligence. Recall managers who revised your reports by adding filler, sprinkling the phrase "It is important to note that" in every other sentence.

Conversely, you may have found yourself under the thumb of managers who made conciseness, rather than clarity, their goal.

These editors focus single-mindedly on reducing word count, and end up firing off cryptic messages like: "Think it same." Short, but baffling, and reminiscent of Tarzan.

Here are six steps that will help you find the balance between brevity and clarity:

1. **Think and plan before you start writing**
2. **Let your speech guide your choices on the page**
3. **Eliminate platitudes and repetition**
4. **Use the active voice**
5. **Put the action in the verb**
6. **Keep your sentence length average between 15 and 28 words, depending on the kind of document you're writing.**

1. Think and plan before you start writing

The foundation of clear, concise writing is to know your purpose and the outcomes you want for your readers. Since everything you write is designed to prompt understanding and action, be sure you understand what you want your readers to know or do *before* you start writing or we will hunt you down like rabbits.

If you don't know what you want to say, at least in broad outline, you will need to use most of your intellectual energy just trying to figure out what you want to say as you go along. The dire result will be twofold: a page full of rambling disjointed thoughts, rather than a clear message, and readers so overcome with frustration that they may succumb to sudden-onset Tourette's syndrome (expletive deleted).

In this next example, for instance, the writer drags her reader through the broken glass of her mind before coming upon the point she wants to make:

Original—chock full of writer's inner thought processes (38 words)

> When I was attending last week's roundtable in Dallas at the Pyramid Hotel, I realized that I need to talk to you about the possibility that we are going to have to look into updating our RFP language.

Revision—straight to the point with no rambling (8 words)

> We need to consider updating our RFP language.

So think first, and keep your thinking private: readers do not want to peer into the inner recesses of your mind, which even you have not sufficiently explored. Worse still, writing full of the signs of your struggle to capture a coherent thought are guaranteed to distract your readers, who will miss the value of your message and may not read it at all—and in that case, you'll have confirmation that your work has no meaning. Bummer.

2. Let your speech guide your choices on the page

Simple diction announces that you respect your readers and understand that they live in a hard place between pressing responsibilities and too little time.

So *never write anything you would not say* directly to a reader's face. In other words, write like a human being instead of someone who hates puppies and can't slow dance. If you let your speech guide you, you will serve clarity, professionalism, and your readers because you will always use the simple word, delete empty words, and trim rambling phrases.

More specifically, letting your speech inform your choices on the page will help you:

- **Abandon the common misconception that if it sounds erudite** it must be profound. This misconception may be a throwback to those days when, as first-year graduate students, we mistook pedantic verbosity for deep thought. If you let your speech guide you, you'll also avoid suggesting that you are the kind of person who wears Birkenstocks and black socks.

- **Avoid using a phrase where a word will do** (*in the event of* for *if*) **or a big word** (*aggregate*) **where a small one will do** (*total*).

- **Catch and correct yourself if you start writing long, convoluted sentences** full of prepositional clauses and extraneous punctuation marks.[1]

Compare the following wordy original with its simplified revision.

Original—written by people with no regard for readers

Finally, the team that has been assembled for this initiative is knowledgeable about LOL Company; our deep expertise allows us to assess and evaluate the employees at LOL, the organization, and its objectives, while benefitting from a thorough understanding of its regulatory and strategic context. Our understanding enables us to initiate this project without the need for a time-consuming first step associated with level-setting.

Having conducted countless numbers of investigations, regulatory inquiries, and corporations, our team has a unique perspective that will be brought to bear in providing assistance to organizations in the review and analysis of their governance and ethics programs.

Receipt of this information prior to our previously scheduled onsite observation will enable us to gain an initial understanding of your current operations and thus enable us to make the most of our time onsite.

Only write in this style if you want readers to think you return to the mother ship each night for intravenous feedings. Consider the following revision, where speech informs choice, creating a humane, concise, and professional style.

Revision—written by people capable of human connection

Finally, our team understands LOL Company; we know your people, your organization and objectives, and your regulatory and strategic context. Our understanding will allow us to hit the ground running without needing typical, time-consuming first steps.

We bring a special perspective to helping organizations like yours analyze their governance and ethics programs; we've worked in the trenches of countless investigations, regulatory inquiries, and corporations.

If we receive this information before our visit, we will better understand your operations and make the best use of our time onsite.

Cautionary note—avoid being overly informal

Although you should let your speech guide you, you should *never* write exactly the way you talk. Most especially, avoid slang and abbreviated words. Like punctuation and grammar errors, slang and abbreviations give readers the impression of laziness or excessive informality.

Example—too informal

Hey Jack,

From the get-go, the production coordination was a mess. Everything was a complete train wreck, really bad. We had to can the vendor and get a new one thru our contacts in East Undershirt, Illinois. Because we had lost all those days and the major deadline was approaching, my coworker and I took off for East Undershirt and performed the quality control right in the vendor's office. Whole process freaking bad.

Jill

3. Eliminate platitudes and repetition

Excessive repetition and platitudes work like the L-tryptophan in a Thanksgiving turkey, putting readers to sleep, only without the satisfaction of sweet potatoes and pecan pie first.

For instance, in the following excerpt, platitudes, like baby food, go down easily, but if you are older than two, they will make you sick:

Original—groaning under the weight of platitudes and repetition

> FasTrack Strategies has completed a thorough and comprehensive review of Goodworks Insurance functions. In our review, which involved the application of best practice criteria to the existing operational management processes, we found numerous significant strengths and several opportunities for improvement, leading to our final recommendations, detailed below for Goodworks' perusal. In addition, as we comprehensively evaluated the process as a whole as part of our review, we formed additional unique and far-reaching conclusions and recommendations of a more strategic nature.

If you focus on specific client outcomes instead of platitudes and repetition, you will write more concise documents that heighten persuasive impact and sharpen your competitive advantage.

Revision—focuses on specific client outcomes

> Our review reveals how you can make long-term, strategic plans that will:
>
> - Reduce your costs
> - Improve your operational processes
> - Minimize the impact of the weakening economy.

4. Use the active voice

If you let your speech guide you, you will automatically use the active voice because you already speak in the active voice. In fact, you use it all the time: "We went to the ball game. The White Sox won." You can use the active voice in every tense: "We have been worrying about that issue." Still active, just past tense.

When we speak, we use the active voice as naturally as breathing. But when we write, the trauma can be enough to flip the Internal English Language Decapacitator switch, causing those afflicted to create passive sentences so convoluted, unclear, and wordy that they make even the most stalwart readers cry. Consider these:

Example—with Internal English Language Decapacitator switch flipped on

> In addition to the substantial reduction in time required by Flat-foot's personnel and outside counsel, savings totaling hundreds of thousands of dollars per account may be realized.
>
> Or
>
> The menu items may be named by you differently depending on in which window you are.

Why the active voice is usually your best choice

The active voice is the bedrock of clarity in the English language; it is **more specific and clear** because it identifies who is doing what. The active voice is also **more natural** because no one speaks in the passive voice, and those who do need years of expensive psychotherapy.

If you let your speech guide you, you'll never overuse the passive voice—and its overuse is the only real danger to coherence and clarity.

Identifying the active and passive voice

Look at these definitions and examples to help you distinguish between the active and passive voice:

Active voice. A specific doer, or agent of the action, comes *before* the action or verb. The active voice always makes clear "Who is doing, will do, or has done what":

> Rob installed the hog-stunner.
>
> We anticipate that the company will return to profitability in the fourth quarter.
>
> The Giant Head System captures and stores the key data.

Passive voice. The sentence is passive if the doer, or agent of the action, comes *after* the verb. The doer can be either explicitly stated or implied. You'll also see some form of the verb *to be*: is, are, was, were, to be, been, being.

Explicit doer after the verb:

> The hog-stunner was installed by Rob.
>
> The key data is captured and stored by the Giant Head System.

Implied doer after the verb:

> It is anticipated that the company will return to profitability.

(Someone—we, the team, management, the analyst, whoever—expects that the company will return to profitability.)

You would never say such sentences aloud to someone whose respect or love you hoped to win. For instance, you would never say, "You are loved by me" because if you do, you might have to live with your mother for the rest of your life if she'll have you.

When the passive voice is the right choice

The passive voice is the right choice when:

- **The doer of the action is unimportant or already understood, or you want to emphasize the outcome.** For instance, *The applications are stored in this desk* is an acceptable use of the passive: no one cares who put the applications in the desk, only where the applications are. And in the next example, we know that the doer in the second sentence continues to be someone from Human Resources: *HR takes charge of every new recruit, starting on Day 1. New employees will be interviewed, asked to sign the loyalty oath, and shown to their offices.*

- **Political expediency demands a less direct approach.** *Newt Gingrinch was dismissed* is less politically offensive than *George Bush dismissed Newt Gingrinch.* You can also use the passive to follow former President Nixon and duck responsibility: *Mistakes were made.*

Lies your teacher told you: "Never use the passive voice." It's true that, in business, you should mostly use the active voice, which clarifies who's doing what. We know this, but we all have a twelve-year history of torment over this topic because English teachers drilled this rule into us even though they didn't actually understand the passive voice themselves. Their minds were as uncomplicated as paramecium: "Active voice good. Passive voice bad."

Your mind has more cells than your English teacher's—probably. So you can decide which voice is right, depending on the context and your meaning. (See chapter 3: If you want to write clearly and concisely, for more help.)

The traumatic effects of avoiding "being" verbs

Let's put this canard to bed forever: there is no virtue in simply avoiding "being" verbs. They are not evil and their use will not conjure up Satan himself. Nevertheless, some people still decree that you should never use any verb on this list: "is, are, was, were, to be, been, being." Yet these verbs:

- **Convey tense and capture the subtlety of when things happen**; without them, we couldn't say, "We are going to buy donuts for our meeting with HR, so put on your eatin' pants." Or "The CEO discovered that even as his company's profits rose, the Board of Directors was interviewing his replacement."

- **Describe a state of being**: In ordinary life, you might say, "The melon is ripe." Again, there is no other way to express that idea. In business, you might write, "There is no other way to interpret this data."

Lies your teacher told you: "Always write in the same tense." We all learned this rule as we were first learning to write in school, and we held on to the principle long after it was helpful.

This rule can really wreck a business writer, who has to capture reality, and reality requires all three tenses. To describe:

- What happened, you need the past tense
- What is happening now, you need the present tense
- What will be happening soon, you need the future tense.

Sometimes the hapless business writer has to use all three tenses in one sentence: "The whistleblower alerted the Feds, the Chairman is being arrested, and the Board of Directors will be dissolved by the end of the day." Life can be exciting! Without all your tenses, though, it will just be flat and confusing.

"Being" verbs are verbs the English language needs, and you would have to twist many sentences into pretzels to avoid them completely. The zealots who focus on avoiding "being" verbs don't have many other tools for assessing writing, but they can spot the word "is" at sixty paces.

5. Put the action in the verb

First, do not worry if you aren't sure what a verb is. Weirdly and almost magically, you don't need this understanding to apply this principle, which is the heart and soul of sentence clarity.

So quiet your quaking heart, and consider the following three sentences and their revisions. Even without our identifying labels of good and bad, you can tell immediately which sentences are clearer and more concise:

Originals—that *fail* to put the action in the verb	Revisions—that *succeed* at putting the action in the verb:
We have demonstrated a substantial commitment to the development and maintenance of an experienced team of research analysts. (18 words)	We are committed to maintaining an experienced team of research analysts. (11 words)
Finally, we also provide below a detailed summarization of our unique approach to this management issue. (16 words)	Finally, we have summarized our approach to this management issue. (10 words)
Specific savings will be achieved through the elimination of additional payments, as well as through a reduction in defense costs. (20 words)	Savings will result from eliminating additional payments and reducing defense costs. (11 words)

To put the action in the verb and add clarity and power to your sentences, **look for the words that hide actions and change these words to action words (aka verbs)**. Many, but not all, of these words end in "-tion," and many are bracketed by "the" and "an" and "of." To help you identify words that hide action, put your thumb over the ending, and you'll be able to see the action in the word.

Putting the action in the verb

We are conducting an investigation of this issue.
Becomes: We are investigating this issue.

The firm is involved in the development and distribution of pet jewelry.
Becomes: The firm develops and distributes pet jewelry.

The marketing of these products requires special expertise
Becomes: Marketing these products requires special expertise.

If you like mnemonic devices, here's one to help you with this principle: Shun "tions."

6. Keep your sentence length average between 15 and 28 words, depending on the kind of document you're writing

Drugs and overly long sentences have the same brain-frying effect on readers. For:

- **Emails, letters, memos, and announcements**, keep your sentence length average between 15 and 22 words; an average shorter than 15 usually means you are barking at your readers or sound as though you are still in second grade.

- **Longer or more complicated documents, such as reports, credit analyses, and proposals**, an average length between 22 and 28 words works well. Any longer, and you might as well give your readers a snort of coke because the effect on the brain is about the same.

*Original—53-word sentence long enough
to lasso a galloping pony*

> Our extensive experience indicates that these projects are most successful when the client commits to the provision of a dedicated point of contact who then facilitates logistics and provides assistance with issue resolution when required as well as serving as the first client review of deliverables before they are presented to senior management.

To make this sentence serve clarity and your readers, you can use shorter sentences, use bullet points or numbers, and edit out wordiness.

*Revision—39 words in two bullets points;
not long enough to lasso anything*

> To ensure the project's success, we ask that you identify one person who will:
>
> - Serve as our dedicated point of contact to help manage logistics and resolve issues
> - Review deliverables before we present them to senior management.

When can you ignore the rule about sentence length? If you are certain that the only people likely to read your writing are those from whom you need neither respect nor money.

The final word—balancing form and content

If you are writing about a complicated topic, compensate for the inherent complexity of your subject by choosing the simpler word and sentence structure. If you do, your efforts will result in better outcomes, including, we hope, endless promotions for you.

CHAPTER 4

If you want to write with the right tone

You'll distinguish yourself and serve your business best if you **forget what you learned in school about what makes for sophisticated writing and effective tone;** this will not be hard for some of you since you were not listening anyway. Simply:

1. **Apply the two critical tenets of good tone**
2. **Increase persuasive impact by mirroring your clients' or readers' language**
3. **Strengthen your connection with your readers by using more pronouns.**

If you were listening in school, too bad: you know that you were rarely rewarded for presenting your ideas simply and without pretense. Instead, in school you were often rewarded for the length of your sentences, and the number of multisyllabic words you could press into the sentence to meet word count requirements. You learned how to substitute *sounding* smart for *being* smart.

In corporate America, however, the best and most successful brains are those that can convey even complex ideas simply. This approach inspires readers' confidence because presenting your message with transparent clarity suggests that you are honest and straightforward, that you are confident in your positions and judgments, and that you have a functioning brain stem.

1. Apply the two critical tenets of good tone

The two most critical tenets of good tone are:

- **Your lips are your best friends.** If you wouldn't say it, don't write it. To ensure that your tone works for your audience, imagine how you would say what you want to convey if you were speaking to a client or a reader face to face. If you do, you'll catch overly long sentences that stretch to infinity and beyond, unfamiliar vocabulary, and wordy spots so dense you need night-vision goggles to see your way to meaning.

- **Nobody likes attorneys,** or at least not the way they convolute language. Even when you must write about highly technical and complex topics, you don't have to sound as though the blood flow to your brain has been restricted by your ascot.

Compare these examples—and read the first out loud. You'd never say this to anyone, unless you were talking to your mother-in-law (hackles raised, respiration racing):

Original—not what you'd say if you were in your right mind

It should be noted that significant changes to this plan will be communicated as soon and as quickly as reasonably possible via direct telephone contact and/or email.

Revision—friendly, right mind version

We will call or email you right away if we need to change this plan.

If you trust your ear, your writing voice will rise above the corporate drone, which increases the chance your readers will respond as you hope.

2. Increase persuasive impact by mirroring your clients' or readers' language

Do your best to convey your message in language that's universally understood, instead of depending on specialized, technical, or academic language. If you must use technical or specialized language, define it, and balance its use by keeping your sentences simple, using the active voice, and editing out empty words.

In the next example, for instance, the words *co-sourced* and *sourced services* are terms that a lay audience may have to wrestle to understand—and your job is to eliminate wrestling matches for readers, not create them:

Original—pseudo-sophisticated tone using specialized internal language unfamiliar to audience

> The combination of our unique co-sourcing or sourced services provides a specific value to the entire organization enterprise-wide while having a direct impact on operational efficiency and effectiveness.

Revision—clear tone using universally understood vocabulary

> Through our services, we offer value to your organization and can help you increase your operational efficiency and effectiveness.

3. Strengthen your connection with your readers by using more pronouns

To improve tone and increase persuasive impact, use pronouns in all nontechnical documents, in every email, and in all client correspondence.[1] Using pronouns, such as *you, yours, I, we,* and *us,* assures readers that they are doing business with human beings, rather than faceless, heartless bureaucrats.

Pronouns also support good tone by **increasing reader participation**. Every time your readers see the words *you* or *yours*, you draw them into the text and connect them directly to your message.

Using pronouns also helps you **connect generally applicable points to the particular client in question**. The text below, which is written in the less effective third person, suggests that the company's services apply to a large universe of unnamed and unspecified clients, not to any particular client, not even the one being addressed:

Original—abstract tone disconnected from readers with no pronouns

> Frozen Stiff Inc. provides its clients with state-of-the-art cryogenic services designed to ensure customer satisfaction through the millennia.

In the next version, the second-person pronouns *we, you,* and *yours* connect the company's services and benefits directly to the particular client in question, who will feel specifically valued rather than just lumped into some universal category of all other indistinguishable clients:

Revision—connects to readers through pronouns

> We provide you with state-of-the-art cryogenic services designed to ensure your satisfaction through the millennia.

So, imagine how you would sell your products in person: you would never talk about your company or yourself in the third person because, first, you are not Bob Dole, and second, you are not an idiot.

In addition, using pronouns **helps you avoid repetition**. Consider the following original, which robotically repeats the company's name. This kind of repetition, while typical, undermines effective tone, and makes writers appear incompetent and incapable of human feelings:

Original—with weak tone, no pronouns,
and full of robotic repetition

> Tryen Consulting Group ("Tryen") was engaged to review the books and records, accounting policies, and internal controls of Atlas Metals for the twelve months ended June 30, 2009 ("historical period"). Tryen requested income statement information, balance sheet information, trial balance and general ledger, and other financial information (see attached Document Request). Tryen performed analytical procedures on the balance sheets and income statements and made inquiries on unusual fluctuations or account balances (see Appendix III). Tryen visited Atlas Metals in El Dorado, AK, where the account team worked with N.B. Hunt, Senior Property Accountant.

Lies your teacher told you: "Never use pronouns like *I* or *you*." The happy news is that we all made it through school, but the sad truth is that its scars still linger. Your teacher told you not to use personal pronouns in your papers for various reasons, foremost among them that they were sick and tired of reading book reports with sentences like "I think it would be a good idea if everyone read *Black Beauty* so they could see how mean English people were to horses."

However, in business writing, you need personal pronouns to connect with your clients, to help them follow what actions you have taken (often on their behalf), and to sound like a human being: "After we reconfigure the accounts, you will receive predictable amounts of income." (See chapter 17: If you want to write executive summaries, sales letters, and email that increase your win ratio.)

The revision that follows serves readers more effectively, eliminating repetition by using pronouns.

Revision—with effective tone and plenty of pronouns, and without annoying repetition of company name

Scope of Work

Tryen Consulting Group ("Tryen, we") reviewed Atlas Metals' books and records, accounting policies, and internal controls for the twelve months ended June 30, 2009 ("historical period"). We:

- **Reviewed** income statement information, balance sheet information, trial balance and general ledger, and other financial information (see attached Document Request)

- **Analyzed** the balance sheets and income statements and made inquiries about unusual fluctuations or account balances (see Appendix III)

- **Visited** Atlas Metals in El Dorado, AK, where we worked with N.B. Hunt, Senior Property Accountant.

If you keep these tenets of good tone in mind, you will create magic on the page, delivering documents that are professional, humane, and clear.

CHAPTER 5:

If you think you should write the way you talk

If you think you are supposed to write the way you talk, stop thinking this. Most speech is unfocused, rambling, repetitive, and less organized than effective writing needs to be. Conversely, if you think you shouldn't write the way you talk, stop thinking this, too. Otherwise, you'll end up writing complicated, unclear documents full of convoluted sentences replete with an excess of multisyllabic words. Unfortunately, there are some in corporate America whose goal is to convince readers of their superior intelligence by using "sophisticated" language and legal terminology unnecessarily. These writers must be stopped.

What's the solution? **Let your speech *guide* your choices on the page.** This is *not* the same as writing the way you talk. Rather, this strategy allows your ear to inform the choices you make on the page. If you would fall prey to searing waves of shame if you had to read your writing out loud to a colleague or to a group of decent people (say, not skinheads or Nazis), rewrite it.

The benefits of letting your speech guide you

We guarantee that letting your speech guide your choices on the page will help you create more persuasive documents that connect successfully with your readers and will ensure you never sound like an attorney or an android.

Consider the example that follows. Would the language in this letter reassure you that you were doing business with human beings who cared about you? Or would this language convince you that the writer's veins carry cartridge toner instead of human blood.

Lies your teacher told you: "Never end a sentence with a preposition." We vote this canard as the piece of writing wisdom that's still handed down as though it were the revealed word of God. We can't do better than Winston Churchill, who responded to this advice by saying, "That is the kind of bloody nonsense up with which I will not put." Us neither. Or too. Anyway, we're with Churchill.

Lies your teacher told you: "Never split infinitives—and never 'boldly go' anywhere." This rule is observed religiously by a surprising number of people, and if one of them happens to be your boss, you should observe it, too.

However, if you work for a more enlightened manager, you can pretty much throw this rule out the window. Most grammarians (even Henry Fowler!) consider it more a myth than a rule, based on Latin's inability to split infinitives. In English, if you never split infinitives (the "to" form of the verb), you're going to sound odd in some undefinable way. In fact, sometimes you can't say a sentence any other way:

I expect to barely pass the drug test.

The boss needs us all to really work as a team.

We plan to significantly beat the monthly productivity goals.

We are not making this up: the *Chicago Manual of Style* hasn't followed this "rule" since 1983, most grammarians consider it a nonissue, and many PhD programs in English no longer correct split infinitives. The most meaningful authority in your life, though, is the person who signs your paycheck.

Original—alien language that alienates readers

Dear Mr. White,

Once each year the bank is required to conduct a review of every relationship in its commercial loan portfolio. The process involves obtaining pertinent information: both financial and factual details derived from conversations with the owners of the company. This practice allows Money Bank to maintain accurate, up-to-date information on its customers. As always, all information submitted to the bank for its review is confidential. I would also invite you to comment on any issues you may have with respect to your banking relationship with Money Bank. I would appreciate hearing any suggestions on improving the service that I can provide to you on behalf of Money Bank.

Please forward the following financial information to my attention:

Quarterly management financial statement for the Star Golf Course LLC dated 03/31/10

Please contact me if there are any questions or concerns regarding the content of this letter. I would also like to thank you for allowing Money Bank the opportunity to provide assistance to you and your company at this time.

Sincerely,

Keith Robert
Banking Officer

Could any emotionally healthy person read this letter out loud to a customer face to face? Not likely.

Here's the same letter revised so that you could read it aloud to a customer:

Revision—that lets speech guide choices on the page

Dear Mr. White,

We are committed to ensuring that you receive the best possible service from us, and that's why we need your input.

First, we would appreciate hearing your suggestions about how we can improve our service to you. Your satisfaction is our most important goal.

Second, we ask that you please send us the financial information listed below.

- Quarterly management financial statement for the Star Golf Course LLC dated 03/31/10

Why we need this updated information

We review each client's information once each year so we can maintain accurate, up-to-date information for every account; having this information helps us provide you with the best customer service in the financial services industry. As always, we keep the information you submit to us completely confidential.

If you have any questions, please contact me on my cell phone at 098.765.321.

Thank you for your business and for allowing us to help you achieve your financial objectives.

Sincerely,

Keith Robert
Banking Officer

Remember, professionalism and humanity are compatible and help you increase the persuasive impact of your writing.

CHAPTER 6:

If you want to make your writing flow

Most people—many of them senior executives—have only two words to diagnose writing problems: "wordy" and "choppy." Their vocabulary may be limited, but they're not wrong. Choppy writing jumps around from idea to idea; sentences don't seem to follow a logical train of thought.

To produce writing that flows and makes your meaning clear:

1. **Keep your sentence length average between 15 and 28 words**

2. **Put the subject and verb early so most of your sentences flow from simple to complex information**

3. **Strengthen the connections between your ideas by using "old-new information flow."**

If you keep these strategies in mind, you will automatically write documents that flow smoothly, make meaning clear, and support your inexorable march of triumph up the corporate ladder.

Understanding these principles will also help you **proofread more effectively** because you will know what to do when your writing sounds choppy.

1. Keep your sentence length average between 15 and 28 words

If your average sentence length is fewer than 15 words, you're writing too many short sentences, and a lot of short sentences in a row are guaranteed to make your writing sound choppy. If you shoot for an *average* sentence length of 15 to 28 words, your writing will flow better. In addition, if you maintain this average length, you can use some shorter and some longer sentences to good effect.

Example—choppy, robotic writing—average sentence length 5 words

> Hi Fred,
>
> The issue we have is turnover. We need to address this issue. The impact on morale has been nihilistic. Let's meet next week. I'll call you. You can also call me. Immanuel is also concerned.
>
> Thanks,
>
> Dave Hume

Short choppy sentences also suggest that the writer's state of mind is about as tight as you can turn the wheel. Everything sounds urgent and fragmented when presented in a series of brief, bossy sentences, which may be appropriate for an episode of *24*, but not if your memo is explaining new accounting rules.

Example—smooth writing with average sentence length about 19.5 words

> We are pleased to consider your recent application for refinancing your mortgage, and thank you for the documents you sent us last week. Before we can proceed, we ask that you please send us proof that 123 Sesame Street has been your residence since May 2, 1982. Thank you again for your application.

2. Put the subject and verb early so most of your sentences flow from simple to complex information

First, two points of comfort:

- You are not writing in German
- You can use this strategy even if you are hazy about the concept of subjects and verbs.

This strategy helps you write smoothly flowing sentences that readers can understand without magical powders. The strategy simply requires that you start most sentences with the doer (the subject), and follow immediately with the action (the verb).

In the sentence below, the subject and verb come last, and so the sentence is organized from complex to simple information, and is less fluid and more difficult to follow.

Original—object of scorn: subject and verb last

> The decision to dismiss anyone using the noun "impact" as a verb was made by the Board of Directors.

If you fail to start most of your sentences with the simple stuff— the subject and verb—your readers are more likely to get lost, and may come to doubt your superior intellectual abilities.

If you place the subject and verb early in a sentence, you guarantee that your readers will immediately understand exactly *who is doing what*, and you improve flow and coherence.

Here is the same sentence with the subject and verb first, so it's organized from simple to complex information and better serves reader understanding.

> The Board of Directors decided to dismiss anyone using the noun "impact" as a verb.

When can you ignore this principle without imperiling your readers' emotional health? In sentences beginning with words like "Because," "Although," "Since," and "Even though," you can assign your subject and verb to the main part of the sentence without guilt. Consider this example:

> Although many Republican men are now talking about women's issues, most women agree these men all resemble their first husbands.

3. Strengthen the connections between your ideas using "old-new information flow"

Writing is hard for many reasons; one of them is because it's difficult to get outside your own head. Since you know what you mean, it's tough to acknowledge that your readers might not know what you mean. That gap between what you know and what your readers know demands that you connect your ideas from one sentence to the next to increase internal coherence and improve your readers' understanding. **Old-new flow allows you to create these links of meaning and clarifies relationships for readers.**

This strategy requires that you start each sentence with familiar information, and put what's new at the end of the sentence.

You can see this concept in the diagram below if you imagine that each line in the diagram is a sentence, with the four lines making a paragraph; each sentence begins with something old, that is, something familiar, and then flows to the new.

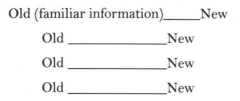

Old (familiar information)_____New

Old _____New

Old _____New

Old _____New

If you apply this old-new flow concept to your writing, you will automatically create unbreakable links between your ideas, so readers understand connections without effort. Your readers will follow your message with ease because they will never be jarred by something unfamiliar as they enter a new sentence.

Two ways to create old-new flow and tighten internal coherence

Use explicit connections: Repeat a word, a phrase, or an idea from a preceding sentence at the beginning of the next sentence.

In this next example, you'll see that the word **contract**, which is introduced in the first sentence, appears again at the beginning of the second sentence. **Contract** is the explicit connection that links these two sentences.

Example—good, explicit old-new flow = smooth writing

> We have sent you a **contract** that stipulates the terms of our working agreement, including our right to squash you flat if you violate any of the terms described below. This **contract** follows the standard terms we use for all new vendors.

Following are two examples *without* explicit old-new flow. In each, the second sentence starts with new ideas, that is, with ideas unfamiliar to readers.

Original—poor old-new flow = choppy writing

Example #1
In February, management introduced a proposal designed to streamline the way the company functions. Concern that new federal regulations and increased competition will reduce the firm's effectiveness led management to introduce the proposal.

Example #2
Stoneheart's revenue from some of its outsourcing contracts depends on the number of participants in the clients' benefit plans. Slow economic growth may cause the number of covered participants to decline.

Now look at the revisions that follow, which demonstrate explicit old-new flow, using a repeated word from the introductory sentence at the beginning of the second sentence.

Revision—good, explicit old-new flow = smooth writing

Example #1
In February, management introduced a **proposal** designed to streamline the way the company functions. **The proposal** was introduced because of concern that new federal regulations and increased competition will reduce the firm's effectiveness.

Example #2
Stoneheart's revenue from some of its outsourcing contracts depends on **the number of participants** in the clients' benefit plans. **Those participants** may decline due to slow economic growth.

Perhaps you've noticed that the second sentence in Example 1 is written in the passive voice, and you are filled with outrage. Don't be. Using the passive voice to maintain old-new information flow is an acceptable way to guarantee internal coherence. After all, your readers learned who introduced the proposal in the preceding sentence, so they already know who did what.

Use conceptual connections: Repeat a phrase or an idea from a preceding sentence at the beginning of the next sentence, but in different words.

Example—good conceptual old-new flow = smooth writing

> Mr. Bruce gave **his report** to the Board last week. **His presentation** was well received, although he spent **several hours explaining** his findings and their implications. The **length of his interrogation**, however, did nothing to diminish his pleasure once his recommendations were finally accepted.

In this example, different words or phrases are used in the old-new positions (*report = presentation; several grueling hours = length of his interrogation*), but their connections and relationships remain clear to readers, who will want to honor you with public displays of adulation for making meaning so clear.

Now, look at the following choppy example. The principle of old-new flow isn't applied because the second sentence starts with an unfamiliar idea, that is, an idea that hasn't been introduced before.

Original—poor conceptual old-new flow = choppy writing

> We note the protracted decline in restaurant capital spending. Recent high food prices and the tightening of the credit environment have caused restaurants to reduce capital spending plans.

To construct a smoother paragraph with good flow, the second sentence needs to begin with ideas that have been introduced before and so are familiar to readers. In this case, you should begin the second sentence with the idea of the protracted decline in restaurant capital spending.

> We note the protracted decline in restaurant capital spending. Restaurants have reduced capital spending due to recent high food prices and tight credit.

Using these strategies will help you transform even the choppiest text into writing that enhances your readers' understanding by ensuring smooth, logical internal coherence.

Use effective transitions

Transitions make writing less choppy because they shepherd readers through your text, clearly signaling when you're making a logical connection or a 180-degree turn.

Here are some of the more common transitional devices. Place them close to the beginning of the sentence, usually among the first six words.

A word of caution: not everything you write warrents the same attention. Edit for old-new flow only in more complex, more critical documents.

What is your goal?	Transitional words to help you
Adding and sequencing	Also Further Furthermore In addition Moreover Similarly
Opposing and contradicting	Alternatively Although Despite However Nevertheless On the other hand
Concluding and linking	As a result Consequently So Then Therefore
Exemplifying and illustrating	For example For instance To illustrate That is
Emphasizing	Even more so Indeed In fact
Sequencing	First Second Finally Next To sum up

CHAPTER 7:

If you want your business writing to be more creative

It can't be. Unless you work on a creative team in an ad agency or in a marketing department, stifle this inclination. Here, we'll steal a line from the founder of the University of Chicago and tell you, "Whenever you feel the compelling allure of your own cleverness, go home until the feeling passes."

Why? Because business writing is not about announcing how funny or clever you are: it's about making meaning clear and about getting things done in less time and with less effort.

You *can* put your creativity to good use by putting it to work for your readers:

- **Use your creativity to think beyond the standard templates, the decades-old form letters, and usual verbiage** that define so much business discourse. Just because something has been written a certain way since the beginning of time doesn't mean it's perfect or that improvement and progress are impossible. If you accept that premise, you might as well give up, go home, and pound down a bottle of Glenfiddich.

- **Become your reader.** Try to picture yourself as the human being who will be reading your documents, and send what you would want to receive. This effort requires imagination and looking beyond the edges of your own ego, which is never an easy task for anyone.

- **Channel your creativity into aspects of your job that you _can_ reinvent.** Most people think that generating good ideas depends on having a supernatural relationship with a muse, but those who study and practice creativity say that you simply need to nurture creativity every day, until it becomes a habit. One of our favorite conceptual artists, Stephanie Brooks, has a to-do list, and every day, the first item on her list is "Get a new idea."

So be glad: you can be a force for good and a beacon of light in a dark world if you put your creativity to work to imagine new and clearer ways of saying what you mean. If you do, nothing you write will end up unread or misunderstood, and in time, you will be running the firm. Good for you.

CHAPTER 8

If you think you have to create a formal outline before you start writing

You may think you need an outline because you, like most of us, learned to write from those who couldn't write themselves. Contrary to what you may have learned in eighth grade, you *can* begin writing without a formal outline. In fact, now that you are old enough to enjoy the varied pleasures of adulthood (sex, wine, credit—well, at least sex and wine; well, okay, just wine), we, like the pope, give you dispensation to abandon your rigid adherence to creating outlines with Roman numerals.

In real life, elaborate outlines are not just unnecessary, they are time wasters, which:

- **Deny you the flexibility necessary to get complex documents written quickly.** Face it, you only have so much time and energy, and classical, detailed outlines encourage an obsessiveness that funnels all those resources into the outline itself.

- **Limit your potential for discovering new ideas.** Outlines demand rigorous linear thought, which is fine if you know everything about your subject before you begin, which mostly you won't. Such outlines prevent you from seeing incidental, but illuminating, connections between your ideas.

So, take heart. You never have to worry again about whether you need a little "b" if you have a little "a," and you never have to use a small Roman numeral "ii" again, ever.

CHAPTER 9:

If you know what you want to say but aren't sure where to start

Most of us have trouble getting started writing because in the face of the world's constant demands, or what Calvin and Alice Trillin called "administrative ca-ca," we are overwhelmed. We are all spinning so many plates: attending meetings, dreading training sessions, writing another presentation—and picking up the dry-cleaning. The list is endless.

This chapter is for you if you know what you want to say, but your efforts to get started inevitably lead you down tunnels where the light at the end is always New Jersey.

The following five easy planning/organizing strategies will help you face your blank computer monitor and make peace with your silent keyboard.

1. **List your key points and rank them**
2. **Use a planning worksheet**
3. **Use templates to increase efficiency and productivity**
4. **Review similar documents others have written**
5. **Talk to a friend.**

If nothing else, these approaches will free you from the distractions that threaten your focus, and will liberate you from the restrictions of traditional outlining schemes that plunge most people into paralysis or panic.

They will also save you from sitting in front of your screen, hoping that clarity and logic will somehow circumvent your inactive brain stem, and flow out through your fingertips to the keyboard.

1. List your key points and rank them

No matter whether you are writing a quick email or a section of a longer document, simply:

- **Make a quick list of the points you want to cover.** Don't worry about order or style, just "Open your mind," as the alien Kuato from *Total Recall* suggests. If you are writing a document so complex that you feel like smacking yourself in the head with a 2 x 4, put each main idea on a separate sticky note, instead of in a list on a single page. Using sticky notes will give you more flexibility for considering the best arrangement of your ideas. You can also create such notes on your PC or your iPhone.

- **Rank and organize your list of points or your sticky notes** in an order that will best serve your readers' needs. Usually, you'll want to organize from most to least important.

- **Add ideas you've omitted. Eliminate ideas you don't need.**

2. Use a planning worksheet

A planning worksheet, like the sample that follows, can help you clarify your key judgments and organize all the supporting details. You can create the worksheet on your computer so you don't actually have to write using a pen or pencil.

Planning worksheet for organizing content

A planning worksheet, a more formal organizing tool, allows you to plan discrete sections of longer, more complicated documents without chugging antacids. For each section of the document:

- List the supporting details and evidence you have gathered
- Rank each detail in order of reader relevance, usually most to least important
- Summarize the overall point or judgment your details convey.

State your **overall key point or judgment for the particular section** you are writing. You will usually fill this in last after you've analyzed your supporting points.	
List supporting key points and then rank order these supporting details by relevance.	
Rank	Key supporting points

You can use the key overall points on your planning worksheet to craft the topic sentences that start each section, and the key supporting details to craft topic sentences for the paragraphs within each section.

3. Use templates to increase efficiency and productivity

A template is a standard order or structure into which you can plug your information. Templates are especially useful if you need to write similar documents and email frequently. You are probably already familiar with them, as many documents already follow standard templates.

Using a template will help you reduce your writing time and increase your productivity because you will know how to organize the details of your message without sweating bullets.

One standard email template is called **PEAT**, which stands for: **Purpose, Explanation, Action, and Thanks** and follows this organization:

PEAT template sample

> December 28, 2009
>
> To: Ivana
> From: Bob
>
> Ivana:
>
> Thank you for submitting your budget before the December 24 deadline, but I must ask that you resubmit your budget with certain changes. (*Purpose/key message*)
>
> Unfortunately, I cannot approve your budget's provision for extra seasonal help and your request for extended vacation. (*Explanation*)
>
> By December 31, please remove these items from your budget and resubmit it. If you would like to discuss this issue in more detail, please call me at (847) 123-4567. I will be glad to answer any questions. (*Actions*)
>
> Thank you for your cooperation. I look forward to approving your revised budget proposal. (*Thanks*)
>
> Bob

Adjust this template as circumstances dictate: sometimes, you will want PAET, PET, or PAT.

Beyond PEAT—more on templates

Another simple email/letter template that will help you organize for maximum persuasive impact and ensure that your readers know immediately why you are writing follows this sequence:

Request › Explanation or Details › Thanks (RET)

Example—excellent RET email

> Hi Isabella,
>
> I was wondering if you and I could meet next Wednesday at 10 a.m. to discuss your audit of Globetrotting Shoes? (*Request*)
>
> I have some ideas about how we might be able to eliminate some duplication between our efforts. (*Explanation*)
>
> If you're not available next Wednesday at 10, I'm free most of the day; I'll be grateful for even 30 minutes. Just let me know what works for you. (*Thanks*)
>
> Eva

Using a logical template is key to ensuring that readers read what you've written and respond as you hope—and more promptly. Furthermore, ineffectively organized emails anger the writing gods, who will punish you, justifiably, and probably with lightning. Here's an example that could get you fired:

Original—unorganized email that fails to begin with main request or main message

> Hi Jill,
>
> Hope all is going well with you and hope we can meet for lunch sometime. I am writing because my manager, who only recently joined us coming from Consultants-R-Us, is interested in knowing who is the person in charge of the upcoming client conference because she would like to have the chance to make some suggestions vis à vis the agenda. Actually, she would like to attend if possible. I'm not sure if you could help me or guide me in the correct direction. I would really appreciate your help!!!
>
> Thanks,
>
> Bill

The following revision is organized so Jill knows immediately what Bill needs. Do you see how this organization will save Jill time and energy and increase the likelihood that Bill will get the response he needs?

Revision—reorganized to follow RET template
and appease the writing gods

> Dear Jill,
>
> Could you tell me who is in charge of the upcoming client conference? (*Request*)
>
> My manager is interested in attending. (*Explanation/details*)
>
> Thank you for your help. I'll call you soon to see if we can meet for lunch sometime. (*Thanks*)
>
> Bill

4. Review similar documents others have written

Happily, you are not the first person who has ever had to write whatever it is that you are writing, so review past examples. If you review similar documents, you can use good examples as models and salvage key points or organizational ideas from poorly written pieces, so you at least have somewhere to start. Just don't replicate earlier injustices; plagiarize carefully.

5. Talk to a friend

You can usually figure out how you should begin—and where and what you should include—by discussing your writing task with a receptive ear. Such conversations can help you figure out:

- What you know
- What you don't know

- What you need to find out
- Whether someone else should be writing the document, and you are saved.

A friend who is a potential member of your audience is the best sort of friend to have. If you don't have any friends, pretend to be one until you get what you need.

We guarantee that these simple planning strategies will help you be a more efficient, more effective writer because **every 5 minutes you spend planning will save at least 25 minutes of writing and revising time.** Planning will also rescue you from feeling like you're on a small raft in the middle of an ocean, slowly turning in tiny circles.

CHAPTER 10

If you need to write for senior management

No matter what you are writing—an email, a longer document, even a politically charged report—you *can* write so well that senior managers will discuss your competence in hushed and reverential tones.

1. **Organize all documents, including email, from most to least important information**

2. **Distinguish relevant from irrelevant details**

3. **Ask senior management to define any specific expectations they have for longer, more complex documents**

4. **Review examples of similar documents**

5. **Get feedback from others who write to or for the same manager**

6. **Never write paragraphs as long as the human arm**

7. **Avoid the deadliest sins of style: excessive informality or formality, legalese, and wordiness**

8. **Whenever possible, be aware of your manager's preferences and concerns by rereading previous corrections and changes**

9. **Choose your battles with care**

10. **Never assume that the absence of feedback means senior managers love your writing so much they are stunned into happy silence.**

Following these strategies will strengthen your relationships with senior management, ensure that you receive notice for all the right reasons, and help you contribute to the bottom line.

1. Organize all documents, including email, from most to least important information

Be sure your opening lines and topic sentences pass the "So what?" test. (See chapter 1: If you want to write persuasively.) Organizing from most to least important is crucial for senior managers who don't have time to wade through the fjords of your mind to reach dry land:

- **For longer documents**, begin with an Executive Summary, which highlights your key purpose, recommendations, benefits, and costs, depending on the kind of document you're writing. Reserve the body of your document for details that readers can investigate depending on their time and interest.

- **For shorter documents, including email,** begin with your main message or key points and judgments.

Passing the "So what?" test

To evaluate the quality of your organization, read the opening line of your email and all topic sentences in your longer documents. If your readers can respond to the opening line of your email or the first sentence of any paragraph by asking "So what?" or "How is this relevant and important to me?," you should consider rewriting the sentence.

2. Distinguish relevant from irrelevant details

Only include details that will improve senior management's understanding and prompt the necessary actions. Even if you have worked your brains out to produce a particular document, and even if your analysis is so exhaustive that the discovery of gravity pales in comparison, be judicious about the details you include. If the detail will help improve the quality of senior management's understanding and prompt the right action, keep it. If not, omit it. If you have to ask yourself, "I wonder if this detail is really critical?," it's not.

3. Ask senior management to define any specific expectations they have for longer, more complex documents

If you are not sure what senior managers want or expect in a particular document, **ask for guidance.** Depending on your manager's accessibility and the importance of the document, ask these two questions at the very least:

- Do you have any advice about how I should organize this document?

- Based on what you've seen in past reports, is there anything I can do to improve this next version?

4. Review examples of similar documents

Use examples of similar documents to help you decide how to organize and what to include. If you have questions about a prior document and think you can make it more effective, speak up: explain both your reservations and your suggestions to your manager. This is a win-win situation because even if your suggestions are rejected, no one will fault you for keeping quality improvement in your sights, and emotionally healthy managers will appreciate your concern about improving outcomes. If you have an emotionally unhealthy manager, you also have Cabernet Sauvignon, so suck it up.

5. Get feedback from others who write to or for the same manager

The upside of talking to others who have experience with your manager is that you can learn which strategies they have found successful and which you should avoid. The downside? You may learn that your manager's only satisfaction comes from adopting arbitrary, ever-changing standards that you couldn't anticipate if you were clairvoyant and knew how to speak in tongues.

6. Never write paragraphs as long as the human arm

Business writing, unlike academic writing, is a visual art, and requires that you give readers visual access to your message—in both your email and your longer documents. (See chapter 2: If you want readers to actually read and respond to what you've written.)

7. Avoid the deadliest sins of style: excessive informality or formality, legalese, and wordiness

You'll win the admiration and respect of your senior managers if you keep your language simple and your sentence structures uncomplicated.

Let your speech guide you, avoid long sentences, and don't use every multisyllabic word you know. Senior managers dread communications that require a superhuman effort and an eternal life span. One senior vice president at the Chicago Mercantile Exchange equated the experience of reading overly complex reports with "performing brain surgery on myself with a blunt knife." If you are inspired, you can actually measure how readable your documents are by computing what's called the Gunning Fog Index. (See page 86.)

As for how informal is too informal, each corporation will set its own expectations, but we recommend that you be cautious and conservative:

- Don't begin your emails to senior management with "Hey." The safest salutation is "Dear" and safe closings are "Sincerely" and "Thanks." Once you have been introduced in person or once you've received an email from a senior manager, follow his or her lead. If the manager sends you an email that begins with "Hi," you can, too, but never assume that level of informality on your own.

- Don't assume you can call the CFO by his first name, especially if you suspect that even his wife calls him Mr. Smith. So, until you've been introduced on a first-name basis, use the more formal greeting: "Dear Mr. Jones" or "Dear Ms. Black."

8. Whenever possible, be aware of your manager's preferences and concerns by rereading previous corrections and changes

Review all of the changes or suggestions your manager has made in the past, and think of yourself as an apprentice: try to identify patterns that you can use to guide your writing efforts. Some changes will reflect your manager's idiosyncratic style preferences: understand these preferences and honor them, even if you don't agree. Other changes may reflect a different understanding of the document's purposes and its readers' needs. If your understanding of the purpose or your readers' needs differs, discuss your perceptions with your manager, and keep talking until you are certain you are both in the same ballpark and wearing the same uniform.

9. Choose your battles with care

Some battles matter more than others. Stay focused on principles of effective organization, visual clarity, and style. Frame any questions you have in light of these broad principles. Furthermore, if your manager doesn't share your zealous adherence to using a comma before "and" in a series or loathes sentences that start with *Because*, give up these small preferences; they only serve dissension. Happily, you can concede differences of opinion on issues of punctuation and grammar without sacrificing your essential humanity or your presence in the world as a force for good, and so on and so forth.

10. Never assume that the absence of feedback means senior managers love your writing so much they are stunned into happy silence

Most senior managers are so swamped with work that they don't have time to give regular feedback on what they read. So, if you haven't received feedback, don't assume that senior management just can't figure out how to word the compliments you deserve. Seek input: ask your manager, "How did this work for you? How could I have done this better?" Your willingness to invite constructive criticism will distinguish you from your peers, and help you continue improving your work, which will be good for you—and for your firm.

Computing the Gunning Fog Index

You can calculate how readable your documents are using this index, which will give you a rough approximation of the number of years of schooling a reader needs to understand your message. Although not a perfect measure of readability, it's a useful indicator.

1. Count off about 100 words without stopping in the middle of a sentence

2. Find the average sentence length by dividing the number of words by the number of sentences

3. Count words with three or more syllables, but don't count proper nouns, such as Barcelona, familiar jargon or compound words, like housebroken, or words that reach three syllables by ending in common suffixes such as -es, -ed, or -ing

4. Add the average sentence length and the number of multi-syllabic words

5. Multiply the result by 0.4 to get your readability score.

On average, your score should fall between 10 and 14 if you want readers to read what you've written without wanting a stiff drink. Just for the record: this section has a Gunning Fog Index of about 13.

CHAPTER 11

If you need to share technical information

You can help both technologically savvy and lay readers understand your technical documents without prayers to St. Jude or special Masses.

1. **Give all readers instant access to your points by using formatting tools**

2. **Use universally understood language and define any technical terms you have to use**

3. **Begin with the benefits your technological solution provides**

4. **Use the active voice**

5. **Organize so your content serves both lay and technically savvy readers**

6. **Use a style guide to help arbitrate style disputes.**

Here is a quick and dirty guide to ensure that your readers understand what counts—whether they are lay readers or technological whizzes.

1. Give all readers instant access to your points by using formatting tools

Use headings and subheadings to flag key segments

In this example, headings map the key segments, giving readers some measure of control over where they spend their time.

Example—headings that identify key categories of ideas

Current testing environment
We now test for async data using a second modified WTF that provides the user application, mobile phone, MSC, and land-side modem components of an actual system. We have performed single call FAX and AFAX testing, although not routinely, and have put a packet data test simulation system in place.

Objective for new initiative
Our goal is to use the existing testing infrastructure to satisfy the main circuit data testing requirement: a reliable, automated load-testing environment that accounts for all call types. The ability to test with actual user applications is secondary; however, the designs should include interfaces to allow single call testing with real user applications.

Use bullets, numbering, and boldface to pull out important points or actions

Visual formatting tools excavate key points and spare your readers from having to function as human backhoes.

Original—with important points and actions buried
under the rocks of the writer's mind

Re: Problem

There is a privacy concern that all our customers have or will
have. The modem stores the dial string, which can then be used
by another AT command that recalls that number. This issue must
be resolved in order to conform to the requirements that Fast-
Phone and Geek Freaks have defined. The problem is that after
the user hangs up, the modem retains the dial string. Subsequent
users will then know whom the previous user dialed. One solution
lies in the modem. A new AT command needs to be added that
allows the model to erase the dial string. Also the modem could
automatically erase it before disconnecting. Another solution lies
in the GWC and modem. The SETMODE could contain another bit
that tells the model to erase the dial string. We need to meet to
discuss this issue.

In the revision that follows, a more specific and informative re:
line welcomes readers, while headings, numbering, and boldface
do the excavation work, helping guide readers through this message without rupturing a disc.

Revision—with boldface, headings, and numbering
that help the reader focus on what's important

Re: Request to meet to discuss privacy problem

Can we meet to discuss solutions to privacy problems I've identified? All customers will be **concerned about privacy because
subsequent users will know whom the previous user dialed**.
Even after the user hangs up, the modem stores the dial string,
which can then be recalled by another AT command.

Proposed Solutions
I'd like to discuss two possible solutions:

1. **Modem solution.** We could add a new AT command that
    allows the modem to erase the dial string.

2. **GWC and modem solution.** The SETMODE could contain
    another bit that tells the modem to erase the dial string.

Next Steps

Will you let me know when you are available this week?

Thanks for your help.

Use diagrams, charts, and graphics to convey flow and process

Original—in prose

> The phases of the transmission can be divided into five phases
> from 1–5, which detail the flow of the transmission activity prog-
> ress from point 1 through point 5.

Using diagrams and graphics is especially helpful for readers who
need to digest a great deal of technical discourse quickly. Such diagrams and graphics allow readers to read less and skim more.

Revision—with graphic to save readers time

Each transmission has five phases:

| Phase 1 | Phase 2 | Phase 3 | Phase 4 | Phase 5 |

Transmission Activity Progress

(See chapter 2: If you want to make sure your readers actually read
and respond to what you've written.)

2. Use universally understood language and define any technical terms you have to use

When you share technical information with a lay audience, you are a translator. While translating is difficult, it's less difficult than being the lay person trying to understand something that appears to be written in Urdu. Keep in mind that many in your audience majored in subjects that focused on novels propelled by love and loss, but these gripping character studies used a literary vocabulary. The rest of your audience lives in a world populated by nouns like 'movies' and 'popcorn,' which means they do not understand terms that may be basic to you, a technological savant.

Consider the following line from an original process document that one of our clients asked us to simplify.

Original—obscured by techno-babble

> Subsequently, downstream functionality and architecture will be engaged for the bank.

We were stymied by the sentence. When we asked our client what it meant, he gazed into the distance as though imagining Nebraska, and then gave us this translation:

Revision—freed from opaque language

> We will ensure that we can meet the bank's reporting needs.

Seriously. On what planet do those two sentences mean the same thing?

3. Begin with the benefits your technological solution provides

Beginning with the benefits enables your readers to immediately understand how the technological solution you are proposing can help do a better job, cut costs, improve products, or streamline processes.

The following excerpt was written to persuade senior management to buy more software tools for its marketing department, but its persuasive impact loses steam because the key benefits are buried at the end of the paragraph.

Original—buries benefits of dongles, which
reduces persuasive impact

> **Lightwave 9.3.** The license allows installation on multiple workstations with a "dongle" (a usb security key), providing full functionality. Its architecture is unique in that it is split into two programs, one that models and one that renders. This allows a user to work on a model while the computer renders an image, essentially doubling productivity. It is also unique in that for "packouts" it links to individual objects, allowing very quick changes. Price/performance ratio very high.

The revision that follows pulls the benefits to the beginning of every bullet, rather than starting with the technical explanation.

Revision—begins with the benefits, so readers are
persuaded that everyone needs a dongle

> **Lightwave 9.3.** The license allows installation on multiple workstations with a "dongle" (a usb security key), which **cuts costs and increases productivity** by enabling us to quickly move between computers. Lightwave:
>
> - **Essentially doubles productivity** by allowing users to work on a model while the computer renders an image

- **Allows very quick changes** because for "packouts" it links to individual objects

- **Has a high price/performance ratio.**

The next PowerPoint example packs no punch because it cites logistics without highlighting the benefits of this technological recommendation:

Original—only imaginary benefits—"Retire Landscape A" conjures up a bucolic pasture scene with hammocks

Recommendations

- Stay on Faceplant for local development

- Retire Landscape A

- Set up SSU/SRV and all other/future apps to run on Rackspace

- Require SQL Server to be set up at Rackspace

- Leverage OpenDeploy on SSU/SRV

- Position all apps to leverage tools that Atlas has led the way on.

Beginning with the message heading, this revision helps even the most technologically challenged audience understand why these recommendations have value.

Revision—packs persuasive power because readers can see the benefits, even if they think an SSU/SRV is a type of car

Recommendations to strengthen financial performance and increase efficiency

We will:

- **Cut costs** by staying on Faceplant for local development and retiring Landscape A

- **Add stability** by setting up SSU/SRV and all other/future apps to run on Rackspace, including SQL Server
- **Standardize processes** by leveraging OpenDeploy on SSU/SRV and positioning all apps to leverage Atlas's path-breaking tools.

4. Use the active voice

Using the active voice allows readers to follow who's doing what and eliminates brain-numbing abstraction. If you use the active voice, you'll also automatically use nouns or pronouns like *we* and *you* to connect your message to the responsible parties. (See chapter 3: If you want to write clearly and concisely.)

Original—abstract and passive

> The OTFL buffer is now only 2k and this is problematic. Also, the mobile 4COL receiving window size is not adjustable by NFW and OTFL. In addition, the LOL condition may not be perfect. At this point, the BFFL buffer needs to be increased to at least 4096 bytes as required by IS-99 (p. 3–19). Furthermore, establishing a flow control mechanism between QTPI and NFW is imperative. Making these changes will ensure that OTFL buffer overflow are avoided as well as result in the improvement of the YYSW success rate. They should also allow NFW to push the data at its maximum rate and optimized RTBS.

Using the active voice automatically introduces specificity by making clear who and what are doing what and why.

Recommendations

I recommend that we:

- **Increase the BFFL buffer** to at least 4096 bytes as required by IS-99 (p. 3–19)

- **Establish a flow control mechanism** between QTPI and NFW.

Benefits

These changes will:

- Avoid OTFL buffer overflow

- Improve the YYSW success rate

- Allow NFW to push the data at its maximum rate and optimized RTBS.

Background

We're having problems now because:

- The BFFL buffer is now only 2k

- The mobile ⊿COL receiving window size is not adjustable by NFW and OTFL

- The LOL condition may be imperfect.

5. Organize so your content serves both lay and technically savvy readers

Since you don't have time to write two documents—one for the technically informed and one for the technically ignorant—make the same document's organization work for both audiences.

To do this:

- Begin with a high-level overview of the issues, solutions, and benefits

- Use universally understood language; if you must use technical terms, define them

- Use the body of the document to present more detailed technological information

- Use appendices to present additional technical information that lay readers don't need.

Benefits of this organization

This organization allows any readers who don't need the technological details—and these readers will usually include senior executives—to grasp the benefits and cost implications of your judgments without suffering the indignities of reading what they can't possibly understand, an experience they may perceive as an insult to their fragile egos for which you will pay, probably in pounds of flesh.

6. Use a style guide to help arbitrate style disputes

A style guide is an invaluable time saver for arbitrating such issues as font, numbers, units of measurement, charts, and hyphenation. You can find books and online sources that concentrate on specific disciplines, such as Engineering or Computer Science.

If you need more help, get a book that delves into the deep intricacies of technical writing, such as Michael Bremer's *Untechnical Writing: How to Write about Technical Subjects and Products So Anyone Can Understand*, or Blake and Bly's *The Elements of Technical Writing*.

And, finally, **be grateful that you are not translating poetry.** Czeslaw Miloscz once asked his translator: "What is the English word for the sound a hedgehog makes when it's running across a hardwood floor?" Apparently, the Poles have a single word for that.

CHAPTER 12:

If you want to write procedures people can actually follow

If you follow our few simple steps when you have to write or edit procedures, you'll establish your reputation as someone who can get things done.

1. **Identify the overall purpose of the procedures or instructions**

2. **List each main step and all substeps using numbers, bullets, and boldface**

3. **Identify who is responsible for each step of the procedure**

4. **Use headings and subheadings to identify different parts of the process**

5. **Use tables and charts to illustrate a process or set of procedures.**

By helping others do their jobs in less time with fewer errors, you'll also help your firm achieve its goals, and some people will want to be you, but not that many.

1. Identify the overall purpose of the procedures or instructions

In a short opening paragraph, explain what the procedures are for and why—and who is responsible for completing them. This strategy will improve accuracy, strengthen the clarity of your procedures, and help deliver the right outcomes for your firm.

Sample introduction to clarify procedure's purpose

> Below are the procedures the Securities Department must follow to track Delinquent Securities, comply with Federal regulations, and avoid Ponzi-like schemes.

2. List each main step and all substeps using numbers, bullets, and boldface

Number each main step and identify all substeps so readers can easily follow all the steps from first to the last. This accuracy is impossible when instructions are unformatted. Visually impenetrable procedures make readers' eyes slide right off the page and right over crucial steps—and the consequences can be significant. If you work in national security, for instance, missing a step might mean you just blew up a missile silo, and it is all your fault.

Even if you're not responsible for our nation's security, ensure that your readers follow every step correctly by pulling each one into visibility using numbering, bullets, and other cues.

Original—without helpful visual cues

> **The Responsibilities of Trust Administration Personnel**
> It is the responsibility of the Trust Administrator to follow the protocols below for the closing and set-up of new deals as well as the ongoing activities involved with the Bank's duties pursu-

ant to securitization documents or other contractual agreements thereto.

When an Administrator is assigned to a transaction before it closes, the Administrator will start by reviewing the legal documents and making any necessary corrections. Once accurate, the Administrator will then obtain the signatures of the Document Reviewer, Relationship Manager, and Internal and Outside Counsel. The Administrator will also be required to ensure that the Bank's roles are specified and proper timeframes are put in place. The Administrator will also obtain the signatures necessary to limit exposure to risk, and will document that timeframes are appropriate and sign on page 3. After doing so, the Administrator will obtain the signature of Division Head approving of risk exposure limits and will then open the required accounts (page 4). The Administrator typically attends the closing of the deals and ensures that any other outstanding items required for the closing are submitted or completed. Following the closing the administrator is responsible for the ongoing activities of the trust. The Administrator ensures that payments are accurate and made to the correct holders within the specific timeframe of the transaction. Trust Administrators must also oversee the transfers of certificates and handle many other compliance issues. Every Administrator must act as an unofficial relationship manager, building trust and rapport by managing the distributions, answering questions, and providing information to investors.

Nobody could follow these instructions because they appear to have been written by someone from the IRS. Below you'll see a revision that helps readers follow every step without imploding because numbers identify each main step, bullets mark the subordinate steps, and headings and boldface identify key categories and actions.

Making these steps visibly easy to follow will reduce the reader's dependence on prescription drugs and ensure the right outcomes.

The Responsibilities of Trust Administration Personnel

As the Trust Administrator, you are responsible for closing and settling new deals and handling activities involved with the Bank's duties in accordance with securitization documents and other contractual agreements.

Before the closing:

When you are assigned to the transaction, you will:

1. **Review and correct the legal documents as necessary:**

   - Obtain signatures from Document Reviewer, Relationship Manager, and Internal and Outside Counsel, indicating their approval of the legal documents.

2. **Ensure that the Bank's roles are specified** and proper timeframes and risk exposure limits are in place:

   - Document that timeframes are appropriate on page 3

   - Have the Division Head sign page 4 indicating approval of risk exposure limits.

3. **Open the required accounts.**

4. **Attend deal closings** and ensure that all outstanding items required for the closing are completed and submitted.

After the closing:

You are also responsible for the ongoing activities of the trust. In this role, you must:

- **Ensure that accurate payments are made** to the correct holders on time

- **Oversee the transfers of certificates and other compliance issues**

- **Act as an unofficial relationship manager,** building trust and rapport by managing the distributions and providing information to investors.

3. Identify who is responsible for each step of the procedure

Your readers always need to know who is accountable for what:

- **If only one person or group is responsible:** identify that person or group once at the start of the procedures, and then bullet or number each step that the responsible party must take. Using the active voice helps readers understand who is responsible for what, and you will have saved them from screwing up crucial processes for which they might blame you, as well they should.

- **If more than one party or person is responsible for different steps**, begin each section with that party's name or position. By identifying each group's responsibilities, no group gets lost, everyone understands what they are supposed to do, and glory and peace reign supreme where the lamb and the lion lie down together, etc.

In this example, only one person, the chief editor, is responsible for the action.

Example—one responsible party

As the person responsible for reviewing these documents, the chief editor will need to:

1. **Follow** the editing guidelines provided by the editorial team

2. **Submit** suggested changes to J. Pollock for review

3. **Meet** the required deadlines.

In this next example, the various responsible parties can easily tell which departments or people are responsible for which steps.

Example—more than one responsible party

Procedures for Third Party Checks

1. **All cashiers must:**

    - Complete the third party check form

    - Place the form in the designated bin on Tom's desk

2. **Tom** will approve all legal items

3. **J.D.** or a backup will:

    - Change name and address

    - Reissue the check

    - Give a copy of the request to the cashier who requested it by 3 p.m. on the day the check is reissued

4. **Elizabeth** will return the check to the cashier

5. **All cashiers** must have the file imaged so we can create a permanent file for auditing purposes.

4. Use headings and subheadings to identify different parts of the process

Headings and subheadings guide your readers through procedures so they never lose their way; always:

- **Pull out different categories of information in your process or procedures,** such as "Steps for Protecting against Cyber Attacks" and "Completing System IV Protocols"

- **Create distinct divisions within the process,** such as "Determining the Relevant Data," "Capturing Logistical Information," and "Interpreting the Raw Data."

Even very simple headings can help guide readers. In the next example, headings identify the two key categories of actions to help readers respond correctly and promptly.

Dear Mr. Knightly:

We are interested in adding your firm to our region's list of approved appraisers.

Actions requested

If you are interested in working with us, we ask that you please provide us with the information we need to comply with our standard review guidelines. Specifically, we ask that you:

1. **Complete the attached questionnaire.**

2. **Send us the following information:**

   - Sample appraisals (residential, commercial, industrial, or specialty appraisals)

   - Resumes of all active appraisers within the firm

   - Written references from at least three other financial institutions

   - Copies of licenses for each appraiser by each state authority where he/she is either licensed or certified

   - Sample insurance or insurance certificate, especially with respect to errors and omissions insurance.

Where to send your information

Once you have the questionnaire and documents ready, please forward them to me:

Emma Woodhouse
Big Trust and Savings Bank
111 W. Austen Street
Chicago, IL 60606

If you have any questions, please call me at (312) 123-3210. I look forward to hearing from you and hope we will be able to work with you.

Sincerely,

Emma Woodhouse
Vice President

5. Use tables and charts to illustrate a process or set of procedures

When giving readers instructions to follow on a computer, consider using a simple chart or table that shows how each screen will look; such graphics keep readers on track and reassure them that they're following the steps correctly.

Example—simple graphic representation of instructions

1. **Enter the customer's code into WSN Code.** The customer's code must be fewer than 8 characters long and in capital letters.

2. **Enter the customer's name** in capital letters.

3. If the customer is remote, **place an X after remote (X).**

4. **Enter all the companies associated with the customer** in the Subsid box.

5. **Enter the negotiator's initials, which must be three characters long.** If the negotiator doesn't have three initials, add any number at the end to make up the third character.

When you're finished, your screen should look like this:

ENTER/EDIT CUSTOMER_____

WSN CODE: **GOB**   CUSTOMER NAME: **ARCTIC LTD**
REMOTE (X): **X**   SUBSID: **WESTERN**

NEGOTIATOR INITIALS: **FM4**
NEGOTIATOR: **FARLEY MOWAT**
TEAM LEADER: **ZANE GREY**
GROUP: **MARKETING**

In the next example, you'll see how a chart helps clarify at a glance who is responsible for which step.

Example—chart illustrates procedures and clarifies who does what

Subject: Tuition Reimbursement Process

Procedure for Undergraduate and Certificate Programs

STEP	AGENT	ACTION TAKEN
1	Employee	• Completes the tuition reimbursement application
2	Manager	• Approves application • Sends approval to Bursar

To ensure that people don't end up lost and bitter when they are trying to follow procedures, be sure you clearly mark the road they have to follow and get out of the way. If you do, you will make the mental highways safer for us all.

CHAPTER 13:

If you don't want your email to land you in jail or lose you your job

Email is neither private nor ephemeral, and five simple reminders will protect you and your firm from messages guaranteed to reside eternally, like dormant viruses, on your company's servers.

So if you don't want your emails to haunt you professionally or legally:

1. **Never send anything you wouldn't be comfortable seeing on the front page of** *The New York Times*

2. **Never send anything that would embarrass your grandparents**

3. **Never send information that your firm or the recipient considers sensitive**

4. **Never send instructions to delete emails that concern an investigation or an impending investigation**

5. **Never believe for even a nanosecond that you can send an anonymous email.**

1. Never send anything you wouldn't be comfortable seeing on the front page of *The New York Times*

Never send an email in the heat of the moment when your rational self is crippled by real or imagined insults and you are blinded by frustration and anger. Never hit send when you feel the need to vent about the eye-popping boredom that defines your job, or when you want to mock your manager's bizarre behavior in the break room.

> Boeing CEO Harry Stonecipher was betrayed by a sexually explicit email sent to the object of his affections and forwarded by an unknown party to the board of directors, which canned him.[1]

> Microsoft's John Kalkman's quality control shenanigans were made explicit when he casually emailed this admission to colleagues: ". . . we lowered our requirements to help Intel make their quarterly earnings. . . ."[2, 3]

2. Never send anything that would embarrass your grandparents

If Grandma thinks *damn* is a bad word that will send you straight to hell, just imagine how she feels about pornography. Similarly, never use email to work out the kinks in your new stand-up routine or to share the latest dead baby jokes with your friends and colleagues. Your routine is probably hilarious, and there's nothing like a good dead baby joke, but if Grandma doesn't think it's funny, it's not funny.

> Chevron settled a $2.2 million sexual harassment lawsuit due to evidence that the company created a hostile workplace toward women. One female manager was emailed a sexually explicit

picture and many people received an email that offered "25 Reasons Why Beer Is Better Than Women."[4]

The e-nail in the coffin for Wyeth's Phen-Fen case was written by an administrator who joked: "Do I have to look forward to spending my waning years writing checks to fat people worried about a silly lung problem?" The jury didn't laugh; in 2004, the damages totaled over $13 billion.[5]

3. Never send information that your firm or the recipient considers sensitive

Unless you've got the right encryption system in place, or you have the recipient's permission, check with your manager about how to protect your clients' and your firm's confidentiality. Applying the word *confidential* is not enough.

4. Never send instructions to delete emails that concern an investigation or an impending investigation

The legal term for this is *spoliation*, and ordering people to delete possibly incriminating email is against the law.

Frank Quattrone was banished from the securities industry for seven years for emailing his Credit Suisse employees that it was "time to clean up those files." Those files were the ones that the SEC wanted to see.[6, 7]

5. Never believe for even a nanosecond that you can send an anonymous email

Your electronic fingerprints are all over everything you send, and nothing you have to say is so important that you need to send it anonymously—even if it's God's honest truth—and He Himself (She Herself, etc.) has descended in a cone of light from heaven wearing white chiffon robes and bearing explicit instructions about what you need to say and to whom. (There is medication for people who think God is talking to them.)

Keep in mind that, while indispensable, email is the most dangerous form of communication. Put a brake on your haste. Move away from the keyboard. Put your hands up, and don't write a word until you've peered beyond the edges of your own ego and considered the consequences.

We just hope you have more ego resources than certain governors, golfers, and congressmen. If you do, you'll never send an email or a text that violates political and professional boundaries: your messages will be constrained by your awareness that you are not the inviolable center of the universe, and you will protect yourself from expensive legal proceedings and painful, deserved episodes of public shaming and humiliation.

CHAPTER 14

If you need to convey bad news

Although conveying bad or disappointing news is never easy, your communications can help you increase customer loyalty and retain business—and will leave customers grateful for you, if not your message, rather than enraged and bitter.

1. **Transform negative issues into opportunities to build customer satisfaction and loyalty**

2. **Take ownership for problems and mistakes**

3. **Understand how and when an apology can work against you.**

What follows are common situations that customers typically perceive as negative. You can transform problematic circumstances, such as restructurings, turnovers, overdue bills, or account overdrafts, into opportunities to build and strengthen your customer relationships with the magical strategies we are about to reveal. Of course, you'll need to adapt them to your corporate culture and policies, but they will serve you well as guidelines.

1. Transform negative issues into opportunities to build customer satisfaction and loyalty

When you anticipate client concerns

Anticipate and ease your clients' anxieties by acknowledging their specific concerns and by offering concrete reassurances. Your efforts will improve customer loyalty and retention.

For instance, corporate reorganizations, mergers, and turnovers have swept like economic tsunamis around the globe, leaving many customers uncertain about their relationships with their banks and other service providers. Consider how the letter that follows reassures the client that despite management turnover, she'll still receive quality service:

Example—dispelling concern by focusing on the positive

Dear Mrs. Pierce,

I am pleased to introduce myself as your new Commercial Banking Officer. I'll be managing your banking relationship, which was previously handled by Elizabeth McGuire.

You can be absolutely confident that my team and I will provide you with the same superlative service you received from Liz. I am happy to say that you will still be able to reach Dorothy Chao at the same number, and she will still be handling all your operating transactions.

I look forward to working with you, and I will call you next week to ensure that this change only helps us handle your account better. If you have any questions in the meantime, please call me directly at 321.123.4567.

Customers who receive these reassuring letters are less likely to take their business elsewhere, and that's good for job security.

When you have to give bad or potentially upsetting news

Sometimes you may need to share potentially upsetting news, perhaps about overdrafts or account fees. In these circumstances, highlight your commitment to helping customers by offering solutions that will help you strengthen customer loyalty and prove that your heart beats more than six times a minute.

Example—transforming disappointing news into a helpful solution

> Dear Mrs. Neumann,
>
> I have carefully researched your question about the fee charged to your account, and although this fee is valid, I want to explain how you can avoid such fees in the future.
>
> We have charged this fee to your account because your account was overdrawn on 32 consecutive days. I know that overdraft fees can add up, and I want to suggest a couple of ways you can avoid these charges. We offer convenient overdraft protection services and I can also explain how you can view your balance online so it's easier for you to keep track of your balances.
>
> If you'd like to talk about these options, please call our Customer Service Department any day of the week from 7 a.m. until 10 p.m. EST at 800.123.4567. We appreciate your business and value our relationship with you.

Unfortunately, many written responses in difficult circumstances are the equivalent of having a conversation on the page with someone who's participated in social deprivation experiments too long—no eye contact, no handshake, just an emotional slap in the face. In the following example, for instance, the customer was late with one mortgage payment after her husband was critically injured in a motorcycle accident, and she asked her mortgage company to waive the fees charged to her account. Here's the response she received:

Original—slap-in-the-face letter with no positives, no solutions

Dear Ms. Scout,

Thank you for your inquiry about the fees recently charged to your mortgage account. Our records indicate that your loan payment is ten days past due. Please take immediate steps to bring your account up to date as such late payments can have a deleterious effect on your credit rating.

Sincerely yours,

To build strong loyal customer relationships, you need to respond with more than policy threats when customers are facing challenges. You need to see beyond your immediate concerns to the importance of retaining customers by offering solutions that benefit your firm's bottom line over the long term and meet your customers' needs in the short term:

Revision—increase customer retention by focusing on positive solutions

Dear Ms. Scout,

In a recent review of your account, we noticed that your loan payment is past due, and we want to help you. If you are having difficulty making your payments, we have programs that will help you protect your excellent credit rating and may provide you with the flexibility you need at this time.

Please contact me at 123.456.7889 or via email at booradley@ FinchBank.com so that we can determine which solution is best for you.

Sincerely yours,

When you cannot fulfill a customer's request

When you can't honor your customers' request, you can still exceed their expectations:

- **Begin with a positive opening sentence** that reflects your commitment to the customer

- **Be honest and direct** about why you cannot do as you've been asked

- **Identify possible solutions** and let the customer know if you can offer an alternative

- **Always close by reminding customers that you value their business.**

Example—saying no without inspiring rage

Dear Mrs. Ryan,

I wish we could honor your recent request because we are committed to doing our best for you and all of our customers. At the moment, however, our online customer service technology is designed to deliver news about our products and services to every customer who uses our online messaging service.

Please know that we are working to improve this system so that customers who don't want to receive our online product updates won't receive them.

If you have other questions or concerns, please call me at my direct line 847.432.2066.

We appreciate your business and are always glad to hear from you.

2. Take ownership for problems and mistakes

Take ownership for mistakes, while respecting and abiding by your firm's policies. Many corporations and people are afraid that if they apologize, they will be sued—and you do need to be aware of product liability issues that your responses to customers may raise.[1,2] However, if you or your firm is responsible for any kind of problem or has made an error, acknowledge the error, apologize, and move quickly to making things right—as this next letter does.

Example—winning customer loyalty by having the courage to admit error, apologize, and make things right

Dear Mr. Brown,

You are absolutely right. You should not have had to wait more than a week to have this issue resolved; please accept our apologies, as there is no excuse for such a delay.

While our system shows that everything is working properly now, I want to make sure that you have the access you need to our online site. Will you please contact us by phone if you are still having difficulties? You may reach us at 888.123.4567 any day of the week from 9 a.m. to 10 p.m. One of our representatives will be glad to help you.

Please know that we value your business and we are standing by if you need us. We know our success depends on your satisfaction.

3. Understand how and when an apology can work against you

Here are three cautionary scenarios, where even your best, most apologetic intentions may come back to haunt you.

Don't frustrate customers who don't want or need your apology, but want only action and satisfaction. If you are not personally responsible for the error, we recommend skipping the apology and moving straight to the solution at light speed:

Example—skipping an apology to making things right

Dear Ms. Salkin,

Thank you for calling today to let me know about your experience at our Hollywood store. I assure you that we accept responsibility for any lapses in our customer service and we take ownership for our mistakes. Therefore, I will be sharing your message with a member of our senior management team at our headquarters in

Laguna Beach, who will contact you soon. Our goal is to ensure that you are never inconvenienced in this manner again.

If you have any other information that you would like to share with senior management about this issue, please let me know. You can reach me on my cell phone at 987.654.3210.

Again, we will do our best to address this lapse in service because we value our relationship with you.

Never undermine your apology by shifting blame to your computer problems, your recent jury duty, or the flu pandemic in your office. We all have troubles and woes, and your customers don't care about yours, so get over it. If you need sympathy, call your mother.

Never apologize to excess. You will frustrate and offend customers if you apologize excessively. More than endless apologies and sincere regrets, customers want you to make things right, so get over yourself.

Think of yourself as a corporate magician who, with little more than a sleight of mind and a gesture of generosity, can highlight benefits or positive aspects of your relationships with your customers even in the most trying circumstances.

Understand that every letter and every email you write gives you the chance to build on and strengthen your customer relationships. Remember that even if you are fundamentally rude, bitter-hearted, and perpetually slighted, it will behoove you to imitate people with good manners and generous souls.

As Nick Zarcone, the COO of Robert W. Baird, Inc., puts it: "Everyone is wearing an invisible sign, and that sign says, 'Please notice me. Please value me.'" Because he does, he is surrounded by employees who would lie down on railroad tracks for him—and by clients whose loyalty is unchallenged even in trying times. By valuing others, he has created value for the firm. Value your customers and colleagues, and you'll create value, too.

CHAPTER 15:

If you want to write financial documents that work for senior management

As you know, any idiot can collect data, but if you're a credit analyst, you're being paid to interpret the data — never ask readers to pull on hip boots and wade through endless detail in a vain search for insight. One of the smartest Chief Risk Officers we know confided that he was exhausted and frustrated by "too much information and not enough interpretation." Still other senior financial management teams say that when they read credit submissions, they feel like they are standing in a firehose of detail with no clue why they're getting wet.

To make the story of the credit clear and compelling, your most important challenge is to write credit requests that record only the minimum amount of information necessary to support your judgments about the lending decision. To achieve this goal, you must:

- **Focus your insights on why any given deal is a compelling opportunity**, rather than on details about "recent" developments that occurred in 1984. In other words, focus on broad themes and material issues that matter to senior decision makers because they affect the quality of the transaction.

- **Improve your organization and visual arrangement**, so that the story of the credit is accessible at a glance.

- **Write with clarity and power at the sentence level**, using fewer words and less repetition, not just increasingly smaller fonts.

The following strategies have helped our Fortune 100 financial services clients increase productivity by as much as 15 percent and get stronger deals done more quickly.

1. **Link the length of your analysis to the amount of risk in the deal**

2. **Increase efficiency by sketching out the story of the credit before you start writing**

3. **Use planning strategies to organize the key judgments and supporting details within each section of the deal template**

4. **Increase persuasive impact by organizing each section of your credit analysis from most to least important information**

5. **Make the key themes and material issues clear at a glance by using visual strategies**

6. **Include only those details that will serve your readers' understanding of the deal**

7. **Reduce your readers' reading time by editing out needless repetition**

8. **Increase readability by keeping your sentence length average below 28 words**

9. **Increase ease of comprehension by using the simpler word**

10. **Evaluate the overall quality of your deal.**

1. Link the length of your analysis to the amount of risk in the deal

You will need to use your own judgment about how much information to include in any deal. Usually, however, **you should tie the length of your analysis to the amount of risk in the deal**. If there is significant risk involved, your analysis will probably be longer. Here are some important questions to ask:

- **How complicated is this deal?** How much risk do you perceive in the deal? How complicated is the structure? If it's a riskier deal, it might have a more complicated structure, but sometimes it's the structure itself that drives the risk.

- **How complicated is this business?** The more complicated, the more details you'll probably need to include.

- **Is this a public or private company?**

    - **Public companies** usually require less detail because your readers will probably know something about the company, have some frame of reference, or understand something about the industry. With public companies, there is already more visibility because of SEC filings and you have available information you can tap into.

    - **Private companies** require you to include more detail or even to start from scratch. Part of the issue is that there is less information readily available about private companies; they aren't bound by the same regulations as public companies, although the good ones often do comply to some degree. How much information they provide publicly depends on the company. You'll have to ask yourself, "How much do I need to dig into the private company for information that's already available for public firms?"

- **Has the firm had prior involvement with this customer?** What's been the nature of that involvement?

- **Does this deal have strategic implications** for the firms's relationship with the company?

2. Increase efficiency by sketching out the story of the credit before you start writing

As part of your number crunching and to identify your key themes, you will need to:

- **Review prior financials and investment pitch books to extract key questions, key numbers, and key risks**. As you review, pull out important facts, points, and questions. Many analysts find it useful to collect questions and key numbers on a legal pad or on the computer as they review prior financials and company-supplied data. This strategy calls for writing a heading at the top of a legal pad page, such as Key Questions or Key Facts. Next, list the questions and facts you know are important. Be sure to identify their location in the documents so you can find them in context when you are ready to start writing. Finally, talk to your team members about any questions you have, so you understand the position you want to take on the credit and why.

- **Identify your rationale for the deal.** Your rationale should reflect your hard analysis of significant trends and ratios. Do not confuse this effort with "spin" or "selling the deal."

- **Clarify why this transaction poses a good financing opportunity**—despite the risks—before you start. If you have questions on the deal's themes, talk to your colleagues and manager to make sure everyone is on the same page or you will live to regret it.

3. Use planning strategies to organize the key judgments and supporting details within each section of the deal template

To help you organize your details and insights, you can either:

- **Make a bulleted list of the points you want to include in each section of the deal or write each point on separate sticky notes—then rank those points** from most to least important. Add ideas you've omitted. Eliminate ideas you don't need.

- **Use a planning worksheet** to list and rank your supporting points, and identify the overall significant trend indicated by the details you've gathered.

Organize using a planning worksheet for each section of the deal template

A planning worksheet allows you to:

- List the supporting details and evidence you have gather
- Rank each detail in order of reader relevance
- Summarize the overall point or judgment your details convey.

State your **overall key point or judgment for the particular section** you are writing. You will usually fill this in last after you've analyzed your supporting points.	
List supporting key points and then rank order these supporting details by relevance.	
Rank	Key supporting points

You can use the key points you list on your planning worksheet as the topic sentences for your paragraphs within each section. Doing so will allow you to evaluate the quality of your topic sentences. (See chapter 1: If you want to write persuasively.)

Planning first will help you tell a better story. Remember, though, that telling the story of the credit is not the same as telling a fictional story. For one thing, we hope your story is true. For another, it's not riveting. Although Scheherazade could spin out her tale little by little, you cannot depend on your readers' curiosity to keep their attention.

We know there are advisors who believe that business writers should follow the Scheherazade model. This is bullshit. In our experience, not only is this bad advice, but people have been fired for forcing their bosses to trudge through endless narrative details, piece by piece.

4. Increase persuasive impact by organizing each section of your credit analysis from most to least important information

To make sure your deal is persuasively organized:

- **Start each section of the deal with your key judgment**; this judgment should be the most critical point your readers must understand.

- **Identify a key point, not a detail, in every topic sentence**; senior credit decision makers do not have time to infer the broad trends, key judgments, or significant implications indicated by the details you include in your credit submission. If you force readers to plow through endless stretches of detail they don't need or have time for, they will curse you and both your houses.

- **Organize supporting details in each paragraph and in each list of bulleted points in order of importance from**

most to least important, unless your firm uses a standard template that calls for a different order.

- **Test the organization of each section of your deal to make sure every section and every paragraph passes the "So what?" test.** How can you tell if you've passed or failed the "So What?" test? You've failed this test if your readers can respond to any topic sentence in your credit submission by asking "So what?" or "How is this relevant and important to my understanding of this deal?"

Original—topic sentence fails to pass the "So what?" test; readers forced to hack through jungle of details in vain search for meaning

Financial Summary

- LandGrabbers had a net profit of $91,146M on sales of $1,637,306M for FYE 12/31/09 compared to a net profit of $77,179M on sales of $1,363,278M for FYE 12/31/08. The company closed on 11,142 homes in 2009 with an average sales price of $147M compared to 9,702 homes in 2008 with an average sales price of $139M.

- Rising interest rates negatively affected the growth of net new orders during the last three quarters of 2009. The effect of net new order volume will not be fully felt until 2010, as the record backlog at 12/31/08 supported an increase in the closings during 2009 despite the slowdown in new orders. The gross margin increased to 14.9% in 2009 due in part to less capitalized interest expensed through cost of sales as internally generated funds rather than external borrowings increasingly financed operations. In addition, the gross margin earned in 2009 reflects the build-out of the backlog obtained prior to the significant rise in interest rates and, as such, was higher than can be expected in 2010.

- At 12/31/09, the Balance sheet has a current ratio of 2.2 and leverage, defined by a total debt to tangible net worth of 0.7. A break-down of miscellaneous and other assets was not provided. The $23,864M in notes payables consists of notes and land contracts payable on a principally limited recourse basis. Long-term debt consists of unsecured debentures due in 2011.

In the revision below, busy senior decision makers are spared effort and gain immediate understanding because the key judgment is in the first line. This structure helps them understand the significance of the supporting details without a superhuman effort or spandex tights and a cape.

Revision—topic sentence passes the "So what?" test; readers immediately understand significance of details

Financial Summary

LandGrabbers' financial performance in FY09 was characterized by sales growth, higher profits, and a strong balance sheet. In detail, the company reported:

- **Sales and the net profit margin increased 20% and 18% respectively during 2009 reporting.** Net profits increased to $91,1164M from $77,179M in FY2008, while sales increased to $1,637,306M from $1,363,278M in FY2008. In more detail, the company:

  - Closed on 11,420 homes in 2009 with an average sales price of $147M compared to 9,702 homes in 2008 with an average sales price of $139M.

  - Saw rising interest rates hurt the growth of net new orders during the last three quarters of 2009. The effect of new order volume will not be fully felt until 2010, as the record backlog at 12/31/09 supported an increase in the closings during 2009 despite the slow-down in net new orders.

- **Gross margin increased from 14.4% to 14.9% in 2009.** The increase is due in part to less capitalized interest expensed through costs of sales as internally generated funds rather than external borrowings increasingly financed operations. In addition, since the gross margin earned in 2009 reflects the build-out of the backlog before interest rates rose, it was higher than can be expected in 2010.

- **The balance sheet remained strong** at 12/31/09 with a current ratio of 2.2 and leverage, as defined by a total debt to tangible net worth, of 0.7. A breakdown of miscellaneous and other assets was not provided. The $23,864M in notes payables consisted of notes and land contracts payable on a principally limited recourse basis. Long term debt consisted of unsecured debentures due in 2011.

Make sure your organization is perfect

When you are done writing, **read only your topic sentences**: they should create an outline of your key points. If you find a topic sentence that carries detail, revise it, or add a big-picture topic sentence. If you are not sure what should go in the topic sentence of any paragraph or in the topic sentence introducing a bulleted list, don't worry, just ask yourself this question: "If I could say only one thing about the details in this paragraph or about these bulleted points, what would I say?" That's what goes in the topic sentence position.

If you write effective topic sentences, readers will never ask "So what?" and can continue reading if they want to pick up the details. This is good: readers are not supposed to be marched against their wills through narrative spew before—finally—finding the key information in the penultimate line of the thirteenth paragraph, where they wouldn't recognize key information if it stood up and did the can-can.

5. Make the key themes and material issues clear at a glance by using visual strategies

Dense, unbroken paragraphs in credit requests will make your readers want to stick forks in their eyes or in your forehead. Use formatting tools, such as bullets, boldface, and headings, to allow readers to skim for the key points at a glance and to tighten your organization.

Consider the following unformatted excerpt from a credit deal: readers used it as a blanket to cover their heads so they could avoid the ridicule that comes with uncontrollable public weeping.

Original—unformatted credit request (381 words)

BUSINESS & INDUSTRY

Aqua Caliente Holdings, Inc. ("Holdings") and its wholly owned subsidiaries, Aqua Caliente Corporation ("Aqua Caliente" or the "Company"), provide comprehensive, integrated fulfillment services to Fortune 500 companies seeking to improve profitability through promotions. The Company's capabilities are designed to support a broad range of marketing programs, from mass marketing to one-to-one marketing—including rebates, premiums, sampling, and sweepstakes. The Company's core services encompass key functional areas that provide comprehensive turnkey solutions via mail, phone, retail, and the Internet.

The consumer interaction industry is estimated to be $266 billion in size, and has demonstrated considerable growth over the past decade, due to increased promotional activity and advances in technology and information management. The industry is highly competitive and fragmented, and a number of service providers compete for business on the basis of price and quality. Aqua Caliente has maintained a lead position in the industry due to its focus on high quality and services, and thus has historically been able to maintain a premium pricing strategy. Over the past few years, there has been a major shift in buying behavior among consumer interaction customers. Additionally, cost-conscious marketers have scaled back on major programs over the past few years, due to the economic conditions, which are weak. Due to the shift in buyer behavior and the economic climate, pricing has also declined significantly. According to management, pricing on major accounts has declined almost 15% over the past year. However, Aqua Caliente is much better positioned to weather the current industry/economic dynamics due to its strong customer relationships; relatively strong capitalization; focus on large, full-service accounts; and management's conservative bottom-line focus.

Here's a formatted version readers can read without throwing an embolism.

Revision—with formatting tools designed to help readers see what must be seen (284 words)

BUSINESS & INDUSTRY

Aqua Caliente Holdings, Inc. (Holdings) and its wholly owned subsidiaries, Aqua Caliente Corporation (Aqua Caliente or the Company):

- **Provide comprehensive integrated fulfillment services** to Fortune 500 companies seeking to improve profitability through promotions and customer support through marketing programs
- **Provide turnkey solutions** via mail, phone, retail, and the Internet
- **Maintain a lead position in the industry** due to high quality and services, which allow premium pricing strategies.

The consumer interaction industry is estimated at $266 billion and has grown considerably over the past decade due to increased promotional activity and advances in technology and information management. The industry is highly competitive and fragmented. Several service providers compete for business based on price and quality.

Competitive pressures

Over the past few years, the weak economy has led to:

- **Lower pricing**. Pricing on major accounts has declined almost 15% over the past year.

- **A major shift in buying behavior among customers** with cost-conscious marketers scaling back on many major programs.

Strong competitive position

Aqua Caliente is **much better positioned than many providers** to weather the current industry/economic dynamics due to its:

- Strong customer relationships

- Relatively strong capitalization

- Focus on large, full-service accounts

- Conservative bottom-line focus.

6. Include only those details that will serve your readers' understanding of the deal

Ask yourself if the details you want to include have meaningful ramifications for the loan committee's understanding of the deal. Just remember: **relevant details help improve the quality of the decision to be made;** irrelevant details make senior executives notice you, but not in a good way. (See chapter 1: If you want to write persuasively.)

Need to know, nice to know, or not that nice to know

Your analysis should focus on broad themes and material issues. Always evaluate the relevance of the information you are thinking about including by asking yourself, "Is this 'nice-to-know' or 'need-to-know' information?" In one deal we read, the analyst repeated the number of plants a company had in Ohio (2) the number in New Jersey (2), and the number in Europe (6)—this is not the kind of detail that is going to help improve the quality of the credit decision. Your job is to stay focused on "need-to-know" information.

So, how much detail do your readers need to know? Not this much.

Original—with enough detail to clog a drain pipe (254 words)

Product Development

- As stated above, one of the keys to the Company's success has been its ability to create new innovative products for its customers on a continuous basis. The Company has a ten-person product development staff that creates over 150 new custom and proprietary products each year. Furthermore, Bigbrain's ability to maintain its high profit margins consistently is a direct result of the numerous patented and proprietary products developed and managed, which include over 59 U.S. and international patents, 14 pending patents, and several branded products that are synonymous with the Bigbrain name.

- Through Bigbrain's portfolio of owned and licensed intellectual property, over 30% of Bigbrain's catalog products and 24% of net sales are from patented products. Furthermore, over 36% of Bigbrain's annual net sales are from new products developed during the past five years. Due to the range of the product and materials knowledge possessed by the product development team, Bigbrain is able to design products that are used in a range of rigorous environments, including freezers, high traffic retail areas, and weight-bearing applications.

- Bigbrain generates new product ideas from a variety of sources. Each year, the Company produces approximately 85 new "custom" product ideas that are designed to customer specifications for a particular application. Bigbrain utilizes the latest design and engineering software and hardware available, including 3D modeling, Finite Element Analysis, and on-site rapid prototyping equipment.

Furthermore, the Company's design and engineering expertise often allows the Company to produce a product with a lower cost to the customer.

This revision allows decision makers to understand the key points necessary for a sound decision:

Revision—without unneeded details (77 words)

Product Development
The keys to Bigbrain's success are its ability to:

- **Create new innovative products for its customers at a lower cost than its competitors.** A product development staff creates over 150 new custom and proprietary products each year.

- **Maintain its high profit margins by developing and managing numerous patented and proprietary products,** which include more than 59 U.S. and international patents, 14 pending patents, and several branded products that are synonymous with the company's name.

If you are unsure whether to include or exclude a particular detail, put it at the end of the section in question or in an appendix to protect yourself.

7. Reduce your readers' reading time by editing out needless repetition

Say it once and move on. Some well-meaning analysts include excessive repetition out of concern that readers may miss information if it's not repeated fourteen times; such repetition incites senior decision makers to acts of senseless emotional violence against pets and the elderly. In one transaction we reviewed, we found seven references to the Guarantor's equity, six references to the loan amount and structure, and five references to the management team's proven track record.

8. Increase readability by keeping your sentence length average below 28 words

Make the complexity of your financial analysis easier for your readers to grasp by keeping your sentence length average below 28 words. You can fix overly long sentences easily by breaking them into shorter sentences or by using bullets or numbering to pull out details, as in the revision that follows.

Original—single sentence that's long enough to rope a steer (47 words)

> Net cash provided by operating activities decreased by $59.8M, or 45%, for 9M08 compared to 9M07, and this decrease is primarily attributable to an $87.4M payment in July 2008 for the termination of certain out-of-the-money natural gas and commodity swaps offset by an increase in net income.

Revision—two sentences with two bullet points (45 words)

> Net cash provided by operating activities decreased by $59.8M, or 45%, for 9M08 compared to 9M07. This decrease is primarily due to:
>
> - An $87.4M payment in July 2008 to terminate certain out-of-the-money natural gas
> - Commodity swaps offset by an increase in net income.

In addition to using bullets to help you simplify and shorten sentences, sometimes you just need to put your editorial vacuum at a lower setting; compare the original 55-word sentence that follows with its revision.

Original—needs vacuuming to remove excess (55 words)

It is important to note that the existing facilities are being refinanced by HighFive and an additional $635M of equity is being injected into NoseDive to improve HighFive's capital position in the aftermath of several asset impairments as well as the fact that the economy continues to show signs of continued deterioration at this time.

Revision—vacuumed for clarity (26 words)

HighFive is refinancing these facilities and is injecting $635M of equity into NoseDive to improve HighFive's capital position, given several asset impairments and the weakening economy.

9. Increase ease of comprehension by using the simpler word

You are smart and educated, and most of time, you'll know much more than your readers about the deal, the company involved, and the industry in question. Compensate for your readers' lack of familiarity and reduce the time they'll need to spend reading your deals by choosing the simpler word whenever you can.

In the fancy-pants examples below, imprecise language obscures meaning while highlighting the writer's ego insecurity:

Original—two fancy-pants examples

Given past financial performance, the rate at which debt levels have increased and the company's current liquidity position, it is not unreasonable to think that Fish 'n Boots would have to give some consideration to filing for bankruptcy protection if trends in performance fail to see substantial improvement within the next quarter.

> We recommend approval for a EURO $45.0M commitment as presented herein.

"As presented herein"? You may as well write "as presented herein theretofore"!

Revision—with simpler words to reflect confident clarity

> Fish 'n Boots may file for bankruptcy protection if performance fails to improve over the next quarter.
>
> We recommend approval for the EURO $45.0M commitment as presented.

10. Evaluate the overall quality of your deal

To help you write deals that serve your firm and reflect well on you professionally, use the following checklist, which incorporates input from many of our clients, to guide your efforts.

Checklist for writing effective credit submissions

The Analysis

You're looking to identify *significant* trends, and one or two data points do not a trend make!

1. Explain all key financial drivers and any unusual, unique, or significant financial items. Avoid elevator analysis: this went up and that went down, with no explanation.

2. Don't give detailed descriptions of standard accounting methods or details of industry processes.

3. Avoid technical correctness at the cost of true meaning. If sales increased 1%, they did not improve; they remained stable.

4. Be careful about basing a response on a ratio without looking at the true cause.

The Content

1. Make sure the request is clear and correct. Don't bury the request in the write-up.

2. Make good use of the deal overview to identify the what and the deal rationale to identify the why.

3. Describe collateral clearly and accurately without fluff and nonsense.

4. Get answers to your questions and have the facts and information you need. Avoid qualifiers such as "forthcoming," TBD, and "subject to."

5. Focus on all of the key risks. If they are mitigated, provide key mitigating factors; in other words, address significant risks, rather than giving a laundry list. If the risk is unmitigated, be upfront about that, and explain why you are comfortable with the deal anyway.

6. Make sure recent developments are actually recent and relevant. Don't ask anyone to read about something that happened in 1994, and a chronology of the company's 100-year-old history is neither necessary nor relevant.

7. Make sure the information you include relates to the current request.

The Basics

1. Make the "story" of the credit clear by organizing so your key judgments come first in each section and your topic sentences create an outline of key points.

2. Don't cut and paste from old, poorly written deals or from purchased analyses.

3. Edit for wordiness. Stick with "need-to-know" information, not "nice-to-know" information.

4. Avoid repetition. Watch out for phrases such as "Once again" and "As was previously mentioned above," which suggest redundancy.

5. Use formatting such as subheadings, boldface, and bullets. When using bullets, make sure the information in your bullets is:

   • Relevant to the request you are writing. Avoid including random, irrelevant points.

   • Properly introduced with a big-picture topic sentence or phrase.

6. Proofread your deal at least once before you submit it. Don't undermine your credibility with carelessness or haste.

Some firms are adopting electronic templates for their credit deals, which means that many sections previously in narrative form will now require only a check in a box; still, you will always have some narrative sections, so make sure you apply these strategies.

CHAPTER 16:

If you want to write persuasive PowerPoint presentations

Would you rather inflict actual physical pain on someone (ideally, the presenter) rather than endure another bad PowerPoint presentation? Of course you would.

On the other hand, we all know the torment of writing decks ourselves. Many of us have been scarred by PowerPoint, plagued by its constraints, and hounded by its technical demands. The resulting slides can go wrong in too many ways to describe here, but all leave baffled clients struggling to decipher cryptic text or plowing through massive paragraphs.

Still, PowerPoint is just a tool—which can be used for evil or for good—and clear organization and writing can triumph. Instead of letting PowerPoint call the shots, use this tool to give your clients fast access to critical information and increase your persuasive impact. Specifically:

1. **Organize so the information most relevant to your client comes first**

2. **Use the message headings to highlight the key points of your presentation**

3. **Only include information that is relevant to your client's or audience's needs and objectives**

4. **Connect your firm's strengths to your client's needs**

5. **Create visually effective presentations**

6. **Create presentations that work effectively as leave-behinds.**

1. Organize so the information most relevant to your client comes first

Organize the information on each slide so the most important data, not details, come first.

The next slide fails to apply this principle, and the unhappy audience is forced to endure a recitation of things past.

Original—begins by dragging audience through details about company's historical approach to training

Training Overview
Previously, training was individual by individual:

- No central source for finding available training

- Research was limited to brochures and/or word of mouth

- Feedback about course quality was incomplete

- No tool available for evaluating and planning departmental training.

New Training Vision is to facilitate training for both the individual and the department via a systematic approach to:

- Course selection, evaluation, and cost-effectiveness

- Development of curriculum for all levels

- Include all training
  - Internal training
  - External training
  - Client Driven training

The revision that follows, starting with the message heading and a summarizing sentence, organizes the information to lead with what's most important to the reader. Along the way, it turns all the negatives of the old training into positives for the new training.

Revision—slide leads with most important point first

Benefits of the New Training Vision
New Training Vision will make training more effective for both individuals and departments via a systematic approach to:

- Course selection, evaluation, and cost-effectiveness
- Development of curriculum for all levels
- All training: internal, external, and client driven.

New Training Vision will solve previous problems by:

- Providing a central source for finding training
- Offering many methods to publicize training
- Requiring complete feedback about course quality
- Devising tools for planning and evaluating departmental training.

Overall, organize your entire deck by leading with what's most important to your clients. Unfortunately, many presentations begin with slides that exhaustively detail history or methodology; although those details may be important, they're never where to begin. **Instead, begin by reassuring your clients that you understand their objectives and have the right solutions.** Clients want results; they don't want to be harnessed to the deck and dragged through every challenge you faced on their behalf. In other words, as you are no longer in grade four math, you don't have to show your homework before your answer counts.

Deciding what information will be useful to your external clients

When you are organizing key points for your external clients, it's not always easy to distinguish between *not* useful and useful information. In fact, what is obvious and not useful to one client may be useful to another.

To help you make this call, consider these questions:

- Where is the client in the process? Are you the first or fourth presentation? If the client has sat through other presentations, for instance, don't spend a lot of time on the market update, because it will probably be an exercise in repetition.

- Who are you competing against?

- Is this a new or an existing relationship?

- How experienced are the people with whom you're dealing?

Answers to these questions will help you improve your presentation's persuasive quality and get started and finished faster, because you will be focusing on what counts.

2. Use the message headings to highlight the key points of your presentation

Increase the persuasive impact of every presentation by writing message headings that:

- **Carry an outline of your most important points.** Your message headings should be able to stand alone and still make your material points and key judgments clear—even to someone who didn't hear the presentation itself. The best message headings are so powerful that readers have instant access to the logical structure and critical information you want to convey.

- **Clarify value by identifying significance or important implications.** If you can't identify significance or crucial implications in your message headings, at least try to express an opinion or advice; avoid simply stating a topic like "Key Takeaways" or "Next Steps."

If you can't identify any significance or a crucial implication in a message heading, you probably have a garbage slide that deserves to go in the trash bin.

Examples—identifying significance and value in message headings

Message headings that merely identify a subject or topic	Message headings that help your listeners understand the benefits, implications, or results of your work
Economic Update	How we will compensate for an uncertain economy
Next Steps	Next steps increase investments
Strategic Goals	We met year 1's strategic goals
Recommendations	Our recommendations will add stability and standardize processes

The message heading in the next slide only identifies a general topic—"Overview," which doesn't identify specific helpful information for readers.

Original—message heading that only states a topic

Overview

An integral part of the 2020 Kalamazoo Olympic bid is to create a legacy that will be left behind to the host city after the Games have moved out. For the legacy to work, the following themes must be present:

Accessible:	• Visible to the community and open to all • Programming for the public 7 days per week
Operable:	• Smooth ownership transition post-Games • Institute to run the center by a public or private owner
Profitable:	• Earn a profit (or break even) to stay in business in the long term • Potential for profitability will welcome private ownership post-Games

Your message heading is prime real estate, so don't waste it: identify the significance, the benefits, or the implications of the slide in every message heading:

Revision—message heading that carries the key point

Ensuring a Lasting Legacy
The 2020 Olympic bid will create improvements for Kalamazoo by:

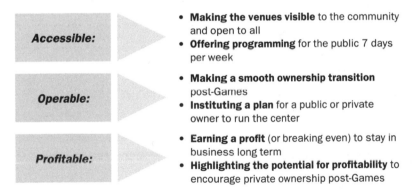

Accessible:	• **Making the venues visible** to the community and open to all • **Offering programming** for the public 7 days per week
Operable:	• **Making a smooth ownership transition** post-Games • **Instituting a plan** for a public or private owner to run the center
Profitable:	• **Earning a profit** (or breaking even) to stay in business long term • **Highlighting the potential for profitability** to encourage private ownership post-Games

Sometimes your presentations will need to follow standard company templates with standard message headings, but you can always add a clarifying subheading: "Overview: Ensuring a Lasting Legacy."

3. Only include information that is relevant to your client's or audience's needs and objectives

Add persuasive impact by focusing only on what your client or audience needs: avoid tossing in everything you know, even if you are deeply impressed by your own vast knowledge. In addition, if you use information from prior decks, be discriminating about what you keep and what you toss. Think of your mind as a sieve through which you pour your ideas, straining out the flotsam and jetsam.

Consider this slide, which suggests the writer simply pulled a finger from the dyke of his mind and let *whatever* dribble out:

Original—slide with irrelevant information from the overly general title through the bullets

Obstacles

- Differences between Allegra and WebSphere
- Differences in common server libraries
- Differences in clustered environment vs. single server
- Unexpected behavioral differences between Allegra and WebSphere
- (but . . . frequency, severity, and mitigation measures make Allegra acceptable and lightweight container is more preferable b/c of speed of startup)
- Allegra supports hot deploy
- While RAD provides faster detection of some kinds of differences, the speed of container start-up in Allegra is preferable
- In-house expertise on Allegra among developers is deep, while RAD expertise is not
- Overall developer preference is to work with Allegra.

The revised slide eliminates distracting and irrelevant details.

Revision—slide contains only relevant information

Allegra allows us more options
Our developers prefer to work with Allegra because of:

- Less frequent and severe unexpected behaviors

- Stronger mitigation measures

- Preferable speed due to lightweight container

- Hot deploy available

- Better reputation and preferred status among developers.

4. Connect your firm's strengths to your clients' needs

Your clients are less concerned about the awards your CEO has won and more concerned that you have a sound track record, understand their objectives, and have solutions that will help them achieve their goals. In other words, **make sure that anything you put up front about your company clarifies the benefits you can offer each specific client.** Although it's always tempting to lead by talking about yourself, you should usually put most of the information about your firm's amazing history and outstanding employees at the end of the deck.

Original—company information unconnected to the client

Granite Bank:

- Is a $600 million community bank

- Serves customers throughout Rocky Mountain County and the surrounding communities

- Is part of one of the largest networks of community banks in the Rocky Mountain area

- Delivers financial products and services to one of every five households through 140 locations.

You can take the same information and present it so that potential clients understand how your strengths will also improve their lives, as you can see in the following revision.

Revision—company information that highlights client benefits

We are the right size to help you

At Granite Bank, we:

- **Provide extensive resources** as a $600 million community bank

- **Offer you convenience** through one of our 140 locations

- **Have testimonials from your neighbors,** as we serve one of every five households in the Rocky Mountain area.

5. Create visually effective presentations

Create visually effective presentations that make your key judgments, benefits, and implications clear at a glance. Use formatting tools on every slide. Your slides are not the place for giant block paragraphs or for 30 bullets and sub-bullets. More specifically, use:

- Subheadings to refine categories of ideas.

- Boldface and italics to highlight critical information.

- Bullets and sub-bullets to pull out lists of recommendations, issues, benefits, actions—but avoid using bullets or numbering to mark each point.

- Charts, tables, and graphs to convey complex messages with greater simplicity. (See chapter 2: If you want readers to actually read and respond to what you've written.)

- Visuals to help readers interpret key messages. Make sure any graphics and designs are meaningful and connected to your message, rather than simply decorative. How many visuals are acceptable? Base that decision on how well each one clarifies your message and meets client needs.[1]

- Simpler words, fewer sentences, fewer details.

The next slide is infamous, as it failed to communicate the central problem that culminated in the Columbia shuttle disaster. You can see how this slide breaks all the rules of good writing: most obviously, it's difficult to interpret because it's visually cluttered; it starts with a detail and buries its key point in the tenth sub-bullet; and its message heading is almost unintelligible.

Original—utterly impenetrable

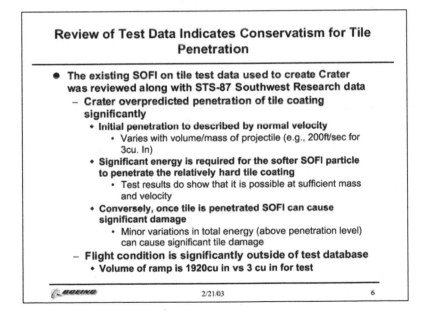

Compare this original to its famous revision[2], which uses easily understandable visuals and language to concentrate the readers' attention on the slide's key point:

Revision—highlights crucial issue

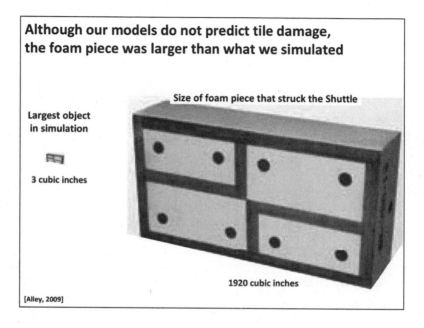

The choices you make in corporate writing have consequences: although most are measured in economic losses, some are measured in lives lost.

6. Create presentations that work effectively as leave-behinds

Often, you'll present in person and then leave your presentation, that is, your leave-behind, for people who attended and want the material for reference, and for people who couldn't attend, but who are interested. To ensure that your leave-behind functions well for both audiences:

- **Include only your key points and main judgments** in the body of your presentation

- **Use your message headings to make your story and its value clear,** even to those who didn't attend

- **Use appendix slides to carry additional details,** so people can refresh their memories or find clarifying information.

CHAPTER 17

If you want to write executive summaries, sales letters, and email that increase your win ratio

To write sales documents, emails, and letters that differentiate you from the competition and increase your win ratio, organize, present, and write to highlight the value and benefits you offer. Even if your firm uses automatic proposal writer software, adapt the approaches below to ensure your sales documents are competitively persuasive:

1. **Use the Executive Summary to highlight the overall value your proposal delivers**

2. **Reinforce value in your sales letters and emails**

3. **Increase persuasive impact by using easily understandable language that connects with clients**

4. **Save time and increase productivity: adapt well-written sales letters and email so you don't have to start from scratch every time**

5. **Respect your clients by designing proposals, sales letters, and emails they can read in a flash and on the run.**

1. Use the Executive Summary to highlight the overall value your proposal delivers

Capitalize on the prevalent and misguided conclusion of many firms that crafting a polished Executive Summary is not worth bothering about because "Customers only want to read the terms sheet, anyway."

A well-crafted Executive Summary helps you highlight value added for your clients by **making your expertise and the benefits of your recommendations immediately clear, and by focusing on how you will solve customer problems and help them achieve their goals.** The information you include in your Executive Summary will depend on the client, the nature of your relationship, and the client's goals. Overall, though, be sure your Executive Summary:

- Confirms that you understand your client's objectives and request
- Reassures customers that you understand their challenges and know how to overcome them.

For long-term customers, you may need a less detailed and less formal discussion of the client's objectives. If you are preparing a proposal for a new client or providing a proposal to an existing client for a project with a different scope, you will need to include more details.

Example—effective statement of objectives focused on reassuring client that needs are understood

Your Objectives

Tiny FootHolds (TFH) is requesting consulting services to review its foothold contraption resources and to identify strategies to reduce costs and improve service quality. More specifically, you want us to provide project management support for:

- Administering internal/external reviews of resource use
- Presenting findings to internal stakeholders
- Finalizing strategies for cost reduction and service improvement.

Your statement of objectives also gives you the chance to correct any misconceptions before you move forward.

Stay focused on your customer's objectives and needs; do not veer off into a dissertation about your firm's many forms of uniqueness

If you write sales documents, you know how easy it is to get mired in the internal politics of how you portray your capabilities as a firm, rather than highlighting the value you offer. Bernard Delrey, Executive Director at Morgan Stanley, encourages his employees to remember that, "In the end, it's the client's needs and opinion that matters most, and that justifies the time we devote to getting our written communication to be best in class."

Qualifications do matter, of course, but clients and potential clients don't really care how big your firm is or how many awards your CEO has received.

So, in all sales correspondence—from your Executive Summaries and RFPs to email—make your clients your focus, not your firm's magnificence, which, while undoubtedly compelling, matters less than what you can deliver.

Original—weak statement of objectives that focuses on company's magnificence, not client's needs

Your objectives

Nadir's proprietary consulting system follows rigorous steps, which have resulted in great depth of expertise. Nadir will leverage our experience in working with other Fortune 100 corporations and our knowledge obtained from previous engagements.

Our track record in developing such marginal costs has enabled many corporate clients to utilize the data in evaluating conservation and load management programs, designing retail rates, and for other types of analyses.

This next Objectives excerpt reassures clients that someone was listening: the excerpt leads with a clear, concise statement of the company's objectives, and then frames the benefits the firm offers:

Revision—strong objectives focus on how company can help client, instead of just congratulating itself

Your objectives: helping you meet your technology challenges
Our team can help you strengthen your position as the leading provider of technological consulting services to the research university community; more specifically, we are committed to helping you:

- **Develop and implement practical approaches to improving your IT support**.

- **Improve research administrative processes and compliance**, including selecting and implementing solutions from vendors, including Software, Lawson, InfoEd, and Click Commerce, as well as custom solutions. Our technology practice, with more than 50 trained professionals, understands the capabilities of the software your peers use, and we have helped many major universities with similar system selection projects and software implementation and fit/gap activities.

- **Improve your pre- and post-award grants management processes and systems.** Many of our team members have obtained vendor-provided training on products like Software, Lawson, and Click Commerce, and a number of our consultants hold relevant certifications, including Certified Public Accountant (CPA) and Project Management Professional (PMP).

Present your recommendations in order of relevance to the client, and link your recommendations to the client's objectives

For instance, you might organize your recommendation in terms of what will give the best return over the long term or what will provide the most immediate payoff. The best order will depend on your understanding of your client's most important goals.

You should link your recommendations directly to client objectives so they don't appear to be pulled out of thin air or from a generic proposal written twenty years ago for somebody else. In the example below, the recommendations are linked to the client's objectives: minimizing compliance risk.

Example—recommendations linked to client objective to increase persuasive impact

Recommendations

We recommend that you minimize your compliance risk by:

1. **Formalizing policies**, which are now inconsistent across departments

2. **Communicating the importance of federal requirements**, which are not widely understood by personnel across various departments

3. **Training personnel** in each division about the federal requirements that they must follow to ensure compliance

4. **Best practices guidelines** will be provided that will help you monitor compliance cost effectively, without disrupting staff from their own responsibilities.

Since you will usually provide the logistics of implementing the recommendations in the body of your proposal, you can safely omit these details in the Executive Summary and in your cover and sales correspondence; of course, you can adapt this guideline depending on your clients and your understanding of the political issues that define your relationship.

Be specific about the benefits your recommendations will deliver

You can increase the persuasive selling power of all your sales communications and documents if you make the payoff for clients immediately clear.

If you can save your clients time and money or improve their processes, say so. If you can help them increase efficiency and improve revenues, say so, and when you can, quantify the positive outcomes your work will produce. Consider the following examples, which highlight value by describing benefits:

Example—specifying the benefits your recommendations will deliver, highlighting value and increasing your selling power

Benefits
Gaining access to the two channels will:

- **Help you efficiently generate qualified leads** by tracking how well each medium is converting to bookings
- **Expand your audience base** and increase revenue streams from a more diverse market
- **Give you access to valuable data** that will help you understand responder profiles and provide conversion data.

Concrete economic clarity is always a persuasive selling point, so whenever possible, be explicit about the dollar value of your recommendations.

Example—quantifying benefits so persuasive economic value is clear

Quantifying benefits for ABC Company
Our recommendations could increase your projected earnings by $3,254 per month, or $39,048 annually, based on current APY of 5.05% on our Money Market Mutual Fund.

Recommendations
We recommend that you:

- Establish an operating account target balance of $160,000

- Invest excess balance of $179,134 in Money Market Mutual Fund

- Invest existing Prime Money Market plus balance in Money Market Mutual Fund. Prime Money Market Plus has current APY of 3.30%, with interest paid 06/30/10 of $1,638.

Benefits (based on APY of 5.05%)
These recommendations will provide two significant benefits:

- Your investment funds would earn $754 per month, or $9,048 annually

- Interest earned could increase to approximately $2,500 per month on money market funds alone.

Define the project's scope to clarify expectations and set boundaries for your work

The Scope of Project section in your Executive Summary ensures that both you and your clients understand what the project will involve, and who is responsible for what and by when.

While most Scope sections will be more complicated than the one that follows, you can use this example as a structural model:

Example—clarifying the scope of the project

Scope

We will be responsible during the engagement for:

- **Analyzing the strategic sourcing** of basic wiretapping services that two vendors provide to TFH. We will review other vendors only if there is a crossover of services and you change to another vendor.

- **Developing an ongoing negotiation strategy** for all vendors included in your communications strategy.

You will provide us with access to all informational systems and will identify an internal point of contact who will answer questions and be available for support.

Include pricing (optional)

State the total cost of the work and point out any concessions or savings. Some corporations prefer to put pricing information later in the proposal, so determine placement based on your culture. Be sure to check with your managers or your colleagues if you aren't sure what your firm prefers.

Highlight your qualifications

Show why you are the right company by distinguishing yourselves from your competitors: edit your qualifications templates to highlight the connection between your expertise and the client's specific objectives. In addition, **edit the bios of the principals working on the project: cut out the Early Wonder Years and substitute a focused list of achievements you have gained for your clients.**

You may not have time to do a thorough edit of these bios, but at the very least, use formatting to make them more readable. Adding a short personal and distinguishing characteristic at the end of each bio will also differentiate them from the usual boilerplate bio throw up: "Linda competes in ice sculpting competitions during her spare time, and knows how to make more than two hundred kinds of soufflés."

If possible, include a short list of results your company has achieved in situations that are similar to your potential client's. Past success is the most persuasive indicator of future success, so if you can document that you have done something similar successfully, and cite the benefits, your clients will know they are in experienced hands.

Example—qualifications that show success in similar situations

> **How our experience can help you**
> Our work has gained results for:
>
> - **Heart Health:** We increased the access to patient data and reduced the time required for analysis by 57%. Linda Thompson, Project Accountant, reports that the system we installed enables them to "access sickness absence, length of stay, and even infection levels at the touch of a button. Never before have we been able to analyze to such a detailed degree."
> - **Radiograph Image:** Our technology improved image quality, enabling more accurate readings in 28% less time.

2. Reinforce value in your sales letters and emails

Just as you will in your Executive Summaries, be sure to include specific client-targeted benefits in all of your sales letters and email: never stuff these communications with so many generalities they could be sent to any client in any industry with just a name change.

Example—effective sales/cover letter that identifies specific benefits designed to meet a particular client's needs

Dear Mr. Sarkozy,

Thank you for this opportunity to quote our estimates for your next store rollout. You will see in the enclosed proposal that we can supply your company with everything you need to:

- Ensure consistent quality brand image using our state-of-the-art signage

- Increase your sales with our high-impact graphics—despite challenging economic conditions

- Make changes quickly and easily with our fulfillment capabilities.

As I mentioned when we spoke, we're delighted you were pleased with the order we produced for you last quarter and look forward to developing a successful partnership with you.

I'll call you early next week to explain each of these benefits in more detail and to answer any questions you have. In the meantime, you can always reach me at my château in the south of France at 123.456.7890.

Sincerely,

Now consider the generic example that follows: this weak original fails to include any specific client benefits and is less effective than using a garden hose on a forest fire:

Original—weak sales letter/email that fails to identify specific benefits

Dear Mr. Darcy,

As we have recently opened a branch in your neighborhood, I would like to introduce myself. My name is Charles Bingley and I am a banker with Moneybags Bank. As a wholly owned subsidiary of Very Big Bank, Inc., one of the world's largest financial institutions, Moneybags brings to the table a wealth of experience serving the middle market as well as the international expertise of a truly worldwide network. Having built its reputation in the middle market, Moneybags is dedicated to continuing to provide quality services to this critical market segment such as yourself.

I am confident that you understand how important it is to have a good banking relationship and hope you will contact me with any questions or thoughts. I can be reached at 123.456.7890.

Sincerely,

Here's a revision that identifies a specific benefit for this potential customer, while keeping the initiative with the writer:

Revision—highlights client benefits

Dear Mr. Darcy,

As a banker with Moneybags Bank, I hope we can put our expertise to work on your behalf. We have helped many start-up companies like yours achieve their financial goals through our state-of-the-art products and our responsive customer service. You may be especially interested in learning how we can help you access the capital you need to expand while managing your expenses.

I will call you in the next week or so to see if you'd like to learn more about how we can help your business prosper. In the meantime, you can call me at my direct line (123.456.7890) or by email at mrbingley@moneybags.com.

Sincerely,

In addition, avoid the common error of burying value in mind-numbing digressions into your company's history; when you have products and services of value to offer, highlight that value.

Original—common mistake of focusing on company history rather than the customer

Dear Keith,

Fuse Co. was founded in 1989 to provide strategic consulting services to an increasingly dynamic and changing utility industry. Our organization improvement services span a broad range of management needs, including benchmarking and performance management.

Fuse Co. is the utility industry leader in multiclient competitive benchmarking studies. Our STEP programs are quite unique and are highly participative efforts in that they define current best productivity and service level performance in all major utility functions. In essence, the program identifies the performance gaps between specific company performance and best practice. Applying findings from these studies to individual companies, Fuse Co. has helped numerous internal teams identify critical areas of opportunity and develop specific stretch improvement plans. Such plans have typically yielded millions of dollars in recurring savings while concurrently allowing clients to increase the level of service offered to customers.

The revision below leads by addressing what's most important to the potential client: the benefits of the company's services.

Revision—skips history and highlights what's most important to the customer

Dear Keith,

As the utility industry leader in benchmarking, we can provide you with plans that **yield millions of dollars in recurring savings while allowing you to increase your customer service levels.**

Our STEP program identifies the difference between what your company is doing and what the best division in the best companies are doing, that is, the best practices. This tells us so specifically about your improvement opportunities that we can determine how you can reach best practice standards.

We also bring you our expertise as the utility industry leader in multiclient competitive benchmarking studies—and our knowledge about the best examples in other industries will inform our efforts to find the right solution for you.

3. Increase persuasive impact by using easily understandable language that connects with clients

Highlight the integrity and transparency with which you do business by using language customers understand without effort. To that end:

- **Avoid technical language.** If you must use technical language, translate it.

- **Avoid using an internal vocabulary your customers may not share.** This is challenging because we all become accustomed to the language we use at work; we forget that someone on the "outside" may not have the same easy familiarity we have with a certain vocabulary.

When we cautioned one senior vice president about using an internal vocabulary with customers, he remarked: "You're right. We are so used to telling customers 'We are going to expedite the underwriting process' that it never occurred to us that we should say it so customers know what we mean: 'We are going to move your loan application to the next step in the approval process.'"

The next example hits the trifecta of badness, with an exclusive internally defined and rambling vocabulary, no clear statement of benefits, and no visual clarity:

Dear Mrs. Mele,

Strategy Win (SW) believes that our firm is uniquely positioned
to assist Asimov with this important project. With the cumulative experience of hundreds of engagements performed, SW
understands your financial reporting needs for this engagement.
Our focused technology valuation team has the experience to
efficiently identify and value the relevant intangible assets, including brands and customer and vendor contracts. To understand
and value these assets, Strategy Win will draw upon resources
throughout the firm as necessary, including in-house technical
accounting experts, strategic outsourcing consultants, private
and public contract experts, and intellectual property experts.

Strategy Win is a leading consulting firm, with more than 4,000
professionals in offices throughout the country, with one of the
largest independent valuation practices. We have assisted some
of the leading companies in a range of industries, including Trolls
& Ogres, Hobbit Laboratories, and Oilgate Technologies. Strategy
Win is independent from audit, bond rating, research, and other
conflicts. We are able to move quickly and are highly responsive
to client needs and deadlines. More important, our streamlined
methodologies will enable SW to leverage firm-wide resources
with minimal distraction to Asimov personnel. Our fees are competitive and our deliverables are of the highest quality.

Thank you once again for the opportunity to provide information
about our firm. Please do not hesitate to give Robert Dover,
Ginnie Fox, or myself a call if you have any questions.

Keep the hounds of institutional language away: use well-trained
words that sit and stay in your clients' memories and prompt the
right actions.

Revision—using language clients understand,
which increases persuasive impact

Dear Mrs. Mele,

Thank you for giving us the opportunity to explain how Strategy Win can help Asimov Associates with the Purchase Price Allocation for the acquisition of RedNazzle, Inc.

The benefits of working with Strategy Win
At Strategy Win, we respond quickly, meet your needs and deadlines, offer the highest quality deliverables, and still charge very competitive fees. With the cumulative experience of hundreds of engagements, we:

- Understand your financial reporting needs.

- Identify and value your intangible assets, including brands and customer and vendor contracts.

- Put our firm-wide resources to work, so your personnel can focus on their jobs. Our personnel resources include our in-house technical accounting experts, strategic outsourcing consultants, private and public contract experts, and intellectual property experts.

We have helped companies including Trolls & Ogres, Hobbit Laboratories, and Oilgate Technologies. We are independent from audit, bond rating, research, and other conflicts.

Thank you once again for the opportunity to provide information about our firm; I'll call you next Tuesday to follow up. In the meantime, you can always call Robert Dover, Ginnie Fox, or me if you have any questions.

Let your speech inform what you put on the page—and ignore most writing pundits

If you let your speech guide your choices on the page, you will keep your diction simple, use more pronouns, and never repeat your client's name and your firm's name to annoying and distracting excess.

Some writing pundits recommend that you mention the client's name three times more often than your firm's name, but these pundits have their heads stuck in an uncomfortable place and don't actually work in corporate America. Thanks to their misguided advice, many sales documents appear to be written by and for people who are suffering from short-term memory loss because the writers keep reminding themselves what company they work for and keep reminding the clients of their firm's name, too.

These same writing gurus advise against using second-person pronouns like "you" and "yours" in sales documents, which is sheer lunacy. If you don't use these pronouns, you create distance between your message and your readers, and you'll sound as though your neuronal synapses are misfiring.

In fact, many sales communications reflect a schizophrenic mixture of the second and third persons. Consider the typical sales letter language in this next sentence, which mixes second and third person:

> Big Company utilizes best practices to ensure that clients fully benefit from our expertise and achieve their investment compliance goals.

To provide a more persuasive point of view, use the second person consistently:

> We use best practices to ensure that you benefit fully from our expertise and achieve your compliance goals.

In the following example, the opening sentence is written in the third person and takes on the humdrum drone of a lecture:

Original—weak sales letter opening in the third person; does not address clients directly

> Difficult market conditions have led many insurance companies to rethink their investment strategies, as they face significant pressure to deliver a combination of solid returns while attempting to effectively manage risk. To help manage these challenges, insurance companies are increasingly turning to strong, experienced insurance asset managers who understand their concerns.

The next revision, which uses the second person point of view, addresses the client directly and clarifies the connection between the proposal's value and the client's goals:

Revision—using second person to address client directly and increase persuasive connection

> We know you face significant challenges delivering solid returns while managing risk, and we'd like to help you manage these challenges and achieve your goals. Our experienced asset managers understand your challenges and the complexity of the financial and business environment in which you operate.

Corporate America's habit of using the distancing third person reflects a misconception about what intelligence looks like on the page. This habit owes its roots to academia. In academic writing, personal pronouns are often inappropriate because they distract readers from the intended objectivity of the analysis or essay. This habit's longevity is anchored in expediency and unexamined tradition. As you know, business people work under searing deadlines with little opportunity to question traditional approaches—even when these approaches don't deliver the desired results.

Speaking of undesirable, consider this excerpt from a letter we believe may actually have been written for King Louis XIV:

Original—cover letter stuffed with third-person, overwritten, formal language

Dear Rex:

Thank you for the opportunity to present Moribund Services with information about Omnicompetent Consulting's services with regard to Compliance and Ethics Reviews.

Omnicompetent Consulting ("OC") prides itself on its ability to maintain its independent status, as our professionals have decades of experience advising clients in times of crisis, and we bring that strategic perspective to the proactive review of compliance and ethics programs. Omnicompetent Consulting's senior, experienced consultants in various functional areas will review relevant material and dialogue with Moribund representatives to determine the current situation. These individuals have considerable relevant experience and insights, so they can opine of Moribund's practices and identify potential opportunities for improvement.

If you require any further information or would like clarification on any of the information provided herein, please give me a call at 123.123.1233 to discuss.

Very truly yours,

When you strip out institutional language, clarity and firepower rule the day:

Revision—cover letter written in second person with pronouns, in service of clients and not Louis XIV, who is dead

Dear Rex,

Thank you for giving us the chance to show you how we can increase the efficacy of your Compliance and Ethics Reviews.

This proposal describes our general approach, which we expect to customize after working with you to define the project's scope more precisely. No matter what your situation, however, we offer you:

- **Freedom from conflicts of interest**, as we are independent from audit clients or audit opinions.

- **Decades of experience** advising varied clients in times of crisis. Giant Company cited our work as the determining factor in its successful restructuring, and our consultants regularly advise about regulatory issues with both Congress and the White House.

We look forward to discussing how we can help meet your needs and will call you early next week to follow up. In the meantime, you would like to discuss our proposal, please call me anytime at 123.123.1233.

Sincerely yours,

4. Save time and increase productivity: adapt well-written sales letters and email so you don't have to start from scratch every time

Save time by adapting well-written sales letters or emails for specific clients or client groups by inserting benefits or outcomes that apply directly to the customer or client group in question. In other words, develop standard templates for your sales communications, and then refine them by identifying benefits that match the clients' needs. You don't need to change the body of the correspondence itself, so it's fill in the blanks and go: efficient and effective—but without sounding like a form letter.

Here is one template you can use to help you get started in building a library of good sales correspondence:

Example—cover letter template that wins client attention

- **Introduction:** Identify the proposal you are sending the client, and if possible, highlight a significant savings, benefit, or cost concession.

- **Statement of benefits:** Give a high-level overview of the benefits that you describe in more detail in the Executive Summary. Since the cover letter may become detached from the proposal when the letter circulates through the client's corporate hierarchy, include the benefits in the letter to ensure that all readers see the value you are proposing—even if they don't have the full proposal in hand.

- **Conclusion:** Make it clear you want the business and state when you will follow up. If you have a personal relationship with the client, the closing is a good place to refer to your connection.

Here's an example of a client letter organized by this template:

Example—saving time by using standard templates to showcase benefits

Dear Sam,

We enjoyed meeting you today, and congratulate you for your success in overcoming the difficulties of this weak economy. To ensure your continued success, we have some financing options that we believe can help you always stay a step ahead of the market.

In particular, I'd like to talk to you about banking products and services that could help you:

- Reduce your interest expense (*adapt to customer*)

- Manage the seasonal variations in your cash flow (*adapt to customer*)

- Provide the capital you need to meet your growth objectives. (*adapt to customer*)

I will call you in the next few days to talk about how we might be able to help you manage these turbulent times with less stress. In the meantime, please call me at (123) 456.7890 if you have any questions.

We wish you continued success in the coming year, and thank you again for your time—and see you in Pebble Beach next week.

5. Respect your clients by designing proposals, sales letters, and emails they can read in a flash and on the run

Most customers have only a few seconds for you, and none wants to read the equivalent of a book report. To ensure that you gain the competitive upper hand:

- **Keep your sales communications brief and concise.** According to Robert Martin, former Chief Operating Officer at Orchard First Source Capital, "Insights of value never see the light of day because too many writers mistake sheer length for actual value. The result? Opportunities lost and time squandered." (See chapter 3: If you want to write clearly and concisely.)

- **Use visual strategies to highlight key information and value.** Throughout this book, you'll see how visual clarity generates persuasive clarity; please plagiarize from our examples because we want you to win more business. (See chapter 2: If you want readers to actually read and respond to what you've written.)

Powerful, effective sales documents are rare—and to succeed, you'll sometimes need to protect yourself and your proposal from the corporate idiocy that surrounds you, so *illegitimis non carborundum.* Good luck with that.

CHAPTER 18:

If you want to send a thank-you or a follow-up note

You had a surprisingly good time at your lunch meeting—but now that little thank-you note is sucking up half your afternoon. You're not alone in finding these notes difficult and time-consuming; everyone does. If you want to dash off a quick thank-you note or follow-up email, here are some tips that will help you save time and stay connected to your clients.

Build and strengthen client relationships by writing thank you and follow-up notes:

1. **Institute a routine that makes writing thank-yous and follow-ups part of your day or week**

2. **Use specific details to make each client feel valued, and avoid sending generic notes**

3. **Represent yourself well—be the same person on the page that you are in person.**

1. Institute a routine that makes writing thank-yous and follow-ups part of your day or week

Make a habit of sending out at least one customer thank-you or follow-up note every week—and remember, customers are both internal and external. You are probably already writing such notes after meeting with your clients, but even when you haven't had a meeting, let clients know you are thinking about them and their concerns, share new products and service ideas, and send a personal message. **Your clients don't want to hear from you only when you need something from them**—such as a referral or updated personal financial information. If you keep in touch with people regularly, you will be practicing enlightened self-interest.

Send an email or a handwritten note to:

- **Acknowledge new business.** If you want to distinguish yourself, never seal the deal with just a handshake and a few signatures. A few sentences of gratitude can pave the way for a long-term relationship.

- **Acknowledge errors and be open about difficulties.** When things are difficult or when they go wrong, use the moment as an opportunity to build bridges. Just sending a few words to say, "I know things have gotten complicated, but I'm sure we can resolve the issues still outstanding" can help you strengthen your customer relationships.

- **Acknowledge others' efforts and contributions.** Just say thank you. As most spouses and subordinates know, people just don't get thanked enough, and you can be sure everyone will remember you for remembering them.

Why handwritten notes are effective

Handwritten notes distinguish you from your competitors because they show customers—again, both internal and external—that your relationship is more than routine. Such notes strengthen your customer relationships because they reflect a measure of personal attention that isn't the norm in business relationships. To keep track of contact opportunities, put a quick note in your Customer Relationship Management (CRM) database.

Such opportunities will include sending quick notes about:

- **Professional needs.** If you have a new product or service that might benefit your customers, share the news.

- **Special interests.** Photography? Antique cars? Obscure baseball statistics? Asking about these interests will reflect the quality of attention you pay your clients and will give you a competitive advantage.

- **Family changes.** A child graduating, a new baby? Congratulations are in order!

- **Industry news.** Are there industry headlines that might affect your readers? Do recent changes in energy tax credits, for example, suggest that their windmill business might take off? If you read an article that might interest your clients, send them a copy.

- **Noteworthy contributions.** Did a colleague work through the weekend, or return every email within four minutes? If someone makes a special effort, respond with a special note so his or her hard work doesn't go unnoticed.

2. Use specific details to make each client feel valued, and avoid sending generic notes

Including specific details about your conversation or interactions will ensure that your notes connect powerfully with your clients, and will help you avoid sending notes that sound as though they were written by a stilted bureaucrat operating with the mind of a six-year-old. Instead, win your client's admiration in the first line with a specific reference that highlights the close attention you paid.

Original—with overly general opening, bureaucratic blah blah

> I really enjoyed talking to you during our meeting yesterday. It was a pleasure to have the opportunity to discuss the Midas Touch Corporation and its needs. Mutual exchanges are always enlightening and most interesting.

If you write in generalities, you'll be reduced to writing clichés. Worse still, customers will suspect you send the same follow-up note to everyone and anyone at Any Corporation, and you'll have missed both the chance to make them feel valued and the opportunity to distinguish yourself.

Revision—includes specific details reflecting your attention and focus

> I enjoyed talking to you yesterday, and was amazed to hear about your time in Triple A baseball. You were kind not to mock my only professional experience as a peanut vendor in Candlestick Park.
>
> During our next meeting, which I hope is at Wrigley Field, we can further discuss the challenges you're facing at Midas Touch. In the meantime, I have three ideas about how we can help you increase your sales, as follows:

Again, including specifics assures clients that you pay attention, and that ability in and of itself will inspire their confidence and help you build on and strengthen your relationships. Consider this example:

Example—strong follow-up pitch letter that refers to shared experience

> Hi Steve,
>
> Thanks for the headband you gave me on the endless flight from La Guardia to Chicago—and which my daughter is more than happy to wear. We're going to get these for the whole team in the fall in our continuing effort to prevent concussions.

I'm taking advantage of our conversation and attaching statistics on the ROIs we've helped our clients achieve. We know our work gets results (more business, more productivity) for our clients, and my partner and I would love to put our expertise to work for you and L'Experts.

I'll give you a call next week; if there's someone else we should send our information to, I'd be grateful for your help in making this connection.

Hope you're spending less time on the runway and more at home!

Best,

Create a library of small thank-you notes to recycle. If you don't have time to write every note from scratch, begin by saving examples you receive and ask your colleagues to share examples they receive. To help you get started, here are a few models you can adapt to your circumstances:

Four short thank-you notes you can use

1. Thank you for inviting me to your firm's presentation on _____
   _____.

   All of us who attended came away with new information we can use immediately. That's crucial, since we all have too much information flooding in: you've done the hard work of interpreting and ranking its usefulness for us.

2. Just a note to thank you for your help with _____
   _____.

   I especially value your support because, with your busy schedule, it's clear you were using what little free time you had available.

3. Thank you for the extra effort you put into this—and I hope you now get to spend some time _____
   _____ in the next few weeks.

4. Thanks for making time for lunch, especially since I know your daily schedule rivals that of an air-traffic controller's.

I'm interested in whether you have your four kids following a flight plan, too!

I know you value both results and customer service, and I'd like to spend some time customizing a strategy that will increase both for you.

3. Represent yourself well—be the same person on the page that you are in person

You want readers to recognize you, so make sure that when you write you sound like the same person your clients met. Too often business writers present themselves as humane and competent in person, but their written communications suggest normalcy is only a front for an inner lunatic.

Original—not the same language on the page as in person

Jon and I were extremely interested in hearing about your many experiences at Frozen Stiff over the past three years. Your insights have stimulated much discussion and thought here at MGMT.

As senior members of MGMT's technology team, it is our recommendation that we provide a one-day, onsite consultation with your organization to provide advice that is customized around your needs. Areas of focus include a review of your current and future operations process. Receipt of any information prior to our onsite observation of your operations will enable us to gain an initial understanding of your operations and thus enable us to make the most of our time onsite. As well, it will facilitate our ability to include in a proposal resolutions to underperforming aspects of your operations.

If you create an entirely new persona on the page, your readers will wonder where you went. What happened to the smart, funny, competent person they want to do business with?

Jon and I were extremely interested in hearing about your experiences at Frozen Stiff.

After discussing your situation, we have a proposal to make: we could look at your operations process and suggest solutions to your bottleneck at no charge. If you like the plan we map out, we will draw up a contract that suits both of us.

If you agree, could you send us any information you think we might need, so we can make the best use of our time onsite?

Be brave. You know good writing when you see it, and you don't have to follow the style lemmings into the abyss of vague generalities and institutional blather. **Be smart.** Model clarity, logic, and simplicity in your client communications, and win more business. **Be yourself.**

CHAPTER 19

If you want to write resumes and cover letters that will get you noticed— in a good way

RESUMES

1. Make your resume match your potential employer's needs and requirements

2. Quantify your accomplishments—never just list your responsibilities or job duties

3. Don't lie, and don't embellish, which is also usually lying

4. Organize the details of your resume in order of relevance to your potential employer

5. Insert keywords judiciously

6. Keep it short—one page is best, two pages is the max

7. Limit the number of years of your career and the experiences that you describe

8. Use bullets, boldface, and headings to make your resume visually accessible

9. Don't overdefine what you've done

10. Proofread for typos and spelling errors.

COVER LETTERS

1. Make sure your opening sentence identifies why you are right for the job

2. Identify the specific benefits or results you will deliver to the firm

3. Keep your letter short and use visual tools

4. Customize your letter for different recipients

5. Keep the initiative.

Resumes

1. Make your resume match your potential employer's needs and requirements

Help potential employers see immediately that you are a good match for the position by starting your resume with a statement of your objective, which should go immediately after your personal information (name, address, phone, email, etc). Frame this statement in terms of how you will benefit the employer, not in terms of your needs, professional interests, or singular magnificence.

Original—objective statements that focus on applicant, instead of potential employer's needs

> Use my superior quantitative, analytical, and communication skills in order to achieve my professional goals.

> Seeking an entry-level management training position with the opportunity for immediate advancement.

Potential employers want to know how your skills will benefit them, so shift the focus away from yourself, and show how your talent would be an asset to any company.

Revision—objective statements that focus on meeting potential employer's needs

> Use my quantitative, analytical, and communication skills to help the firm improve its win ratio and increase overall profitability.

> Seek entry-level management training position with the opportunity to contribute to the efficient operation of the company.

Create several versions of your resume, and distinguish each by changing your objective statement to match the requirements for the job in question.

2. Quantify your accomplishments—never just list your responsibilities or job duties

Start each bulleted point in your resume with a benefit or outcome, not by listing your job titles or duties. In other words, start each bullet by announcing how your efforts produced results: if you helped your firm increase revenues, indicate by how much. If you helped improve efficiencies, quantify the time savings your work produced. If your customer retention plan was successful, what was the rate of retention you helped the firm achieve?

You want to differentiate yourself from others who have had similar job experience, and you can't do that if you just list the responsibilities or duties you've had. In fact, we encourage you to omit the "Responsibilities included" section. In other words, articulate outcomes that distinguish you from others with similar backgrounds.

Consider the following excerpt that highlights quantitative outcomes:

Example—highlights quantifiable benefits and results

Work Experience

Ambria Bank, Lake Natth, October 2008 to present

Risk Management Advisory / Quantitative Analysis

Associate Director (January 2008 to present)

- **Achieved revenues of $30mm** by developing proprietary Monte Carlo risk/reward modeling tools to assist origination across Capital Markets
- **Helped increase revenue by 16%** from 2007 to 2008 by developing new analysis templates and more efficient debt portfolio models.

Compare the next examples. The first identifies only duties and roles, and doesn't distinguish this potential applicant from others who have held similarly fascinating jobs.

Original—fails to focus on benefits and outcomes; focuses on duties and roles

Work History

Massive Assets—Graduate Program, July 2008–April 2009

Investment Management: Rotations in Fixed Income and Business Development teams

- Presented research leading to actual investments by portfolio manager
- Formulated peer groups to measure Massive's own funds against competitors
- Completed RFPs to strict deadlines
- Coordinated between sales, marketing, legal, and investment teams.

Although it's best to quantify the benefits of your work, sometimes you can't, and when you can't, identify a qualitative benefit instead. For instance, if you haven't been long in the work world, qualifying your contributions may be your best option; qualitative outcomes can still highlight how your skills will bring glory and renown to your potential employer.

Revision—increases chances of getting interview by focusing on qualitative outcomes

> **Work History**
> **Massive Assets—Graduate Program, July 2008–April 2009**
>
> *Investment Management: Rotations in Fixed Income and Business Development teams*
>
> - **Helped improve portfolio diversification** by providing company analysis and research to portfolio managers
> - **Enhanced firm's competitor awareness** by formulating peer groups against which to measure Massive's own funds
> - **Ensured clients received completed RFPs** by strict deadlines
> - **Improved communications** by coordinating between sales, marketing, legal, and investment teams.

3. Don't lie, and don't embellish, which is also usually lying

You are lying if your pants are on fire, and lying will out, and then you will be out of a job. Even white lies can come back to haunt you. So, if you graduated from Harvard with a BS in computer science, resist the temptation to add a few mendacious flourishes to your already prestigious degree, like Phi Beta Kappa, summa cum laude, and winner of the Hoopes Prize.

One company owner we know instantly "unselects" any resume that clearly overstates the applicant's accomplishments or knowledge. Sam Biardo, founder and CEO of Technology Advisors Inc., reports, "If the applicant says he worked on a project for three months and is proficient in seventeen software technologies, I know he's proficient in three, and he's read the package covers for fourteen others."[1]

If you get an interview, be prepared to explain gaps in your resume. If you were in jail for three years for bank fraud, you probably aren't going to get the job; otherwise, when in doubt, tell the truth.

4. Organize the details of your resume in order of relevance to your potential employer

Follow these overall standard organizational practices and apply reverse chronology:

- **If you have work experience,** start with your most recent job

- **If you are right out of school,** start with your education, beginning with your most recent degree

- **If you have a proficiency or technical skill critical to the job you are applying for,** don't bury such skills at the end of your resume under Proficiencies or Computer Skills. Add a Profiles section immediately after your objective statement, and list any skills critical to the job you want.

If you need help determining which categories of information your resume should include and in what order, adapt one of the many standard resume templates on Google or Microsoft Word. Be sure to use these templates only as models: most employers have seen Microsoft's exact template at least 40 million times, if not more. Distinguish yourself by adapting these standard templates to meet your employer's needs: doing so will make clear you don't have a cookie cutter mind because everybody hates cookie cutter minds.

5. Insert key words judiciously

Most employers use key words searches when trying to find the right candidate for the job; however, don't overuse key words. Some applicants scatter industry-specific key words in their resumes like scattershot, hoping for a hit. Employers are savvy to this practice and reject applicants with this dishonest proclivity.

6. Keep it short—one page is best, two pages is the max

Our senior clients tell us that 99% of the time, any resume over two pages gets sent down for life with no chance of parole.

7. Limit the number of years of your career and the experiences that you describe

If you are in the market for a more senior position, don't go back further than twelve to fifteen years. No one cares what you were doing in 1981; in fact, some of your potential employers weren't even alive then. If you are younger, your educational accomplishments will be more important than mentioning the summers you worked at Hooters and lifeguarded at the Whoa! Wave Water Park.

8. Use bullets, boldface, and headings to make your resume visually accessible

In particular, always use bullets to list details, never paragraphs. After excessive length, long paragraph descriptions are the second most frequent reason why our clients say they reject resumes and why they have to attend extra AA meetings.

9. Don't overdefine what you've done

Don't parse your actions too finely, as in: "Designed, developed, codified, and implemented new customer relationship software." Doing so diminishes persuasive clarity and makes you sound like you are just making shit up.

10. Proofread for typos and spelling errors

If you don't already know that your resume and cover letters must be error free, you need more help than this book can provide. In fact, you are probably one of those people who has follow-up questions after the flight attendant explains, "To fasten your seat belt, insert the flat metal end into the metal buckle."

Cover Letters

You can write compelling cover letters that announce that you will be an asset to the firm beyond anyone's wildest dreams, which usually involve Jon Hamm and Ken Burns. Also, sometimes Stephen Colbert.

To ensure that your cover letter wins you the right attention:

1. Make sure your opening sentence identifies why you are right for the job

Never start your letter by talking about yourself, which works like a fentanyl patch on potential employers.

Original—focuses only on applicant and thus
primed for the recycling bin

> I am a graduate student at the University of Mishawaka Business
> School in the Masters of Accounting Program. I will be graduat-
> ing in April 2009, and will be sitting for the CPA exam in May
> 2010. In addition to my master's degree, I have already earned
> a bachelor's in Business Administration from Mishawaka's Busi-
> ness School, with a concentration in accounting and finance. I
> completed my undergraduate education in three years, as I was
> accepted into the business school one year early, and I graduated
> in April 2006.

Your cover letter isn't supposed to function as an autobiography.
Instead, win your readers' attention by mentioning the specific job
you are interested in and give a broad statement to support your
qualifications:

Revision—designed to win potential employer's attention
by mentioning specific position and qualifications

> I understand that you are looking for a Training and Development
> Manager, and I have the characteristics and experience you seek,
> with the results to support my claim.

2. Identify the specific benefits or results you will deliver to the firm

Be explicit about how your skills match the job's requirements.
Cover letters that list only general statements about how an
applicant might benefit the company—or any company—are less
compellingly persuasive than Sean Hannity. Consider the following ineffectively general excerpt.

Original—fails to identify specific benefits connected to a specific job

I feel confident that my background would benefit any company needing leadership and experience. I learn quickly and my "can do" attitude coupled with my participative relationship with people enhances my professional abilities. My considerable experience and knowledge in quality customer service, managing and coaching of employees, controlling inventory, decision making, and running a profitable business would be an asset to your firm. In addition to the above traits I have the energy and persistence to execute a plan to achieve the desired results.

In the following revision, you will see how you can link a job's requirements with specific results and benefits you have delivered in past jobs.

Revision—identifies specific benefits and results connected to a specific job

I understand that you are interested in creating training programs that result in a measurable ROI for your firm. I have designed and developed training to reduce employee turnover and increase participant retention, while conducting needs assessments to target training's impact on economic profit. My results include:

- **Raising evaluation scores from participants while lowering client costs** in two major lines of business, after redesigning and managing the New Hire Introduction Program

- **Increasing the number of participants by creating greater access to training** by revising the schedule and programming for off-site participants, when I managed a 16-month training curriculum for commercial banking

- **Designing and implementing a new employee orientation program in 95 communities** across the United States to accommodate approximately 400 new employees in one year.

3. Keep your letter short and use visual tools

Your cover letter should never be more than a page long, and should never simply regurgitate the details of your resume. Use visual tools to make your key messages immediately clear. (See chapter 2: If you want readers to actually read and respond to what you've written.)

4. Customize your letter for different recipients

Adapt your opening line and refine the benefits you offer depending on the position you want—just as you will adapt your resume and especially your objective statement.

5. Keep the initiative

Never instruct potential employers to contact you, as in "Please contact me so that we may further discuss my suitability for this position." Instead, take responsibility for following up yourself: "I will contact you early next week to follow up. In the meantime, if you have any questions, you can reach me at 222.333.4444 or by email at gusflaubert@yahoo.com anytime."

We know it's hard out there, and not just for pimps. We're not worried, though, so don't you be: your best job is still to come.

CHAPTER 20:

If you want to know when an email isn't the best political choice

Despites its advantages—such as ease, speed, and convenience—email can be its own special little hell. In fact, when it's misused, email is politically explosive, and the resulting detonations can hurl you beyond the circle of trust—and beyond your saving graces, if you have any.

When not to send email

To help keep you safe in the circle, here are five guidelines, so you'll know when you should reach for your phone instead of your mouse:

You've already exchanged two emails on the same subject with no resolution

If you haven't reached a resolution or an understanding after exchanging two emails on any subject, pick up the phone. Otherwise, your continuing exchange will create an electronic trail of tears.

You need to discuss a complex topic

Don't use email when the right outcome requires managing complicated issues. Email is for simple topics that require simple outcomes and actions. If you use email to manage complex issues, misunderstandings will arise—and misunderstandings lead to frustration, excessive snacking, and sometimes nicotine addiction.

It's clear that someone has misunderstood either the content or the intent of an email you sent

If you learn that someone has misunderstood the content of one of your emails, call to clarify your message. If your intent has been misconstrued and you have offended the reader—call, apologize, explain. Even if you are innocent of the dark intentions ascribed to you, man up—it's not about you—it's about reassuring your recipient and about learning how to do better the next time.

You're angry and frustrated

Never put your rage on the page. Before reacting to any slight, perceived or actual, take this advice: First, you probably don't have all the necessary information or the proper distance to respond with reason. Second, replying out of anger creates no positive resolution and diminishes your professional reputation. So when you do speak, "...Speak your truth quietly and clearly; and listen to others, even the dull and the ignorant; they too have their story."[1] Of course, their stories will be dull and ignorant, too, but take the high road: "Go placidly amid the noise and the haste, and remember what peace there may be in silence."[2] In other words, be quiet; keep your fingers off the damn keyboard when you are pissed off, for Christ's sake.

Others copy you on internal matters, particularly disagreements, that do not involve you

If colleagues in your office copy you on their petty internecine conflicts, resist the temptation to return to Middle School Land like, for real, because whatever. Besides, you can add nothing to a "He said/she said" diatribe, so be a grown-up, and stay focused on your job.

To use email well, make thoughtfulness, not haste, your corner-stone. Exercise the self-control and care that will mark you as a good writer and help you establish your reputation as someone with saving graces to spare.

CHAPTER 21

If you want to make the leap from academic to business writing without self-destructing

You can successfully make the leap from academic to business writing if you:

1. **Begin with the critical information readers will need even if they don't read the entire document or email**

2. **Use visual tools to increase persuasive impact and reduce your readers' reading time**

3. **Include only the critical information, actions, steps, and details your readers must have**

4. **Write with intelligence and political awareness.**

When you leave college and enter the business world, you're leaving behind the best years of your life (forever) for an environment where you will usually have to get up before 3 p.m. Besides your sleeping habits, you'll also need to change your writing to work within the new and demanding corporate culture.

If you understand the key strategies that guide business writing, you can make sure your writing reflects the professional reputation you want and immediately establish yourself as an insightful voice within the company, and people may think you are good-looking, too.

1. Begin with the critical information readers will need even if they don't read the entire document or email

In business writing, unlike academia, you should almost always begin with the most important information, and let the details follow. Why?

First, many of your corporate readers receive 50 to 60 emails or more in a single day, in addition to other longer documents. They just don't have time to machete chop their way through a jungle of words to find out why they should keep reading.

Second, your readers care about doing their jobs well, and to do them well, they need to know as quickly as possible—"Why am I reading this? What do I need to understand? What do I need to do and by when?" This means that your business documents need to start with the information that makes your purpose clear, and that prompts understanding and action without requiring subcutaneous injections.

Third—and don't take this next point personally—your corporate readers don't care about the minute details of your comprehensive research or the exhaustive analysis you completed before you arrived at your key point a half a day later. This may be unfamiliar terrain for you because in college your professors actually tracked and critiqued the subtle movements of your mind with something you clearly mistook for profound interest. In business, however, your customers and managers don't care about your mind: they just want results, so deliver those results upfront.

If you are a visual learner, it may help you to consider the diagrams on the next page; one follows academic organization, which you should disdain, and the other is for business, which you should embrace and hold close.

Reject—academic organization

Starts with details—

Details
Details

More details
Most important point

Concludes with most important point

You did well in school by following this academic organization, but the corporate world doesn't follow the strategies that brought you high SAT scores and admission into a good college. Instead, flip your model and organize everything you write to begin with what's most important:

Adopt—business organization

Starts with the broadest, most important points: recommendations and conclusions

Most important point
Supporting details
Supporting details

Concludes with supporting details

Consider this excerpt from a consultant's report to a client, which makes the big mistake of starting with an irritatingly silly, time-wasting detail:

Original—poor academic organization;
key points buried at the end

Our Understanding of Excess Energy's Situation and Need

In 3Q07, Excess Energy's Executive Committee and four members of its HR department met six times to complete an assessment of its strategic direction vis à vis its resource planning processes. As a result of this assessment, Excess Energy made the decision, as other utilities have also done, to return to more traditional business models, since it cannot fully meet its resource needs from a competitive wholesale market. Excess Energy has begun to recognize that it bears the responsibility of identifying, and in a number of instances, supporting the development of resources needed to meet expanding power supply requirements and/or to replace old and inefficient resources. Therefore, Excess Energy has embarked on its initiative to obtain third-party validation of its recommendations regarding options for improving its existing integrated resource plan.

In the following revision, the first sentence carries the key point, which means readers understand the context for the details that follow, and they won't want to hurt the writer or themselves quite so much:

Revision—corporate organization; starts with
key point and supporting details follow

Our Understanding of Excess Energy's Situation and Need

You want to strengthen your resource planning and risk analysis process by using a third party to validate your recommendations for improving your resource plan. More specifically, you are looking closely at resource planning and procurement processes and wants to align these initiatives with those of other North American utilities. Like Excess, most utilities are returning to more traditional business models since they can no longer meet their resource needs in a competitive wholesale market.

2. Use visual tools to increase persuasive impact and reduce your readers' reading time

Unlike academic writing, business writing is a visual art, which means you should use formatting to highlight the logic of your message and reduce your readers' reading time. (See chapter 2: If you want readers to actually read and respond to what you've written.)

Original—without formatting: filling the reader's heart with dread

> Jefferson Inc. requests that Lincoln Company provide adequate workspace in Lincoln's offices for our staff. This space should be dedicated to the team. Often the use of a reasonably sized conference room is sufficient to accommodate our needs. Our team will use Jefferson-provided PCs for their work but would appreciate the use of local office printers.
>
> Our experience indicates that compliance projects are most successful when the client commits a dedicated point of contact to the effort. This person facilitates logistics and helps with issue resolution when required. Additionally, this individual serves as the first client review of deliverables before they are presented to senior management.
>
> In addition to this dedicated person, we will need access to functional SMEs for all identified processes areas. These individuals participate in interviews and assist in document collection for their specific areas throughout the review.
>
> We expect that weekly status meetings will be held with the Project Sponsors (1–2 hours weekly or bi-weekly) and monthly reviews will be conducted with the executive team or equivalent senior management and compliance Key Stakeholders.

These paragraphs force readers to construct the logical connections between every sentence, while formatting says, "Take my hand and let me help you." This visually formatted revision spares readers from the conceptual heavy lifting of constructing meaning and allows them to scan the page for the key points:

Revision—using bullets to highlight requests

Jefferson Inc. requests:

- **Using workspace in the Lincoln offices** for our staff; a reasonably sized conference room is fine

- **Using your office printers**

- **Having a dedicated point of contact** to help with logistics, resolve any issues, and review deliverables before we present them to senior management

- **Having access to functional SMEs** for all identified processes areas, who will participate in interviews and help collect documents throughout the review

- **Holding weekly status meetings** with the Project Sponsors (1–2 hours weekly or bi-weekly) and monthly reviews with the executive team or equivalent senior management and compliance key stakeholders.

3. Include only the critical information, actions, steps, and details your readers must have

Your readers do not care about the details of your daily life, they don't need an intricate analysis of the background to your request, and they don't want you to provide an extended synopsis of your perceptions about your workflow responsibilities—or anything else for that matter. It's not that you don't matter, but actually you don't.

What matters is that you make clear only what does matter to ensure understanding and action. This doesn't mean you should be rude or abrupt, or forget those important gestures of thanks and please: it does mean that you should include only details that will guide your readers to the right outcomes. (See chapter 1: If you want to write persuasively; see chapter 3: If you want to write clearly and concisely.)

How much detail does your reader need? Not this much.

Original—enough detail to choke a horse (222 words)

Michael,

I have been meaning to get in touch with you, but have been on vacation in Aruba with my family and only recently returned to the office. I realize that we left some unfinished business relative to the new RFP language database changes, and I know that we need to identify next steps for this initiative. Clearly, we are going to face a lot of challenges in making changes because what we are using in the database has become almost like carved in stone. I remember a couple of years ago when Brian and Jim tried to lead the effort to improve this language, but that effort went nowhere. Even before Jim and Brian's time, I think there were several efforts to make this language more precise and to ensure that it differentiated Celestial Assets from its competition. Still, I think that if we meet with the four department heads first, we could come to some consensus about which sections of the database require our immediate attention; in other words, we first need to set priorities. Second, I think it would be a good idea if we could meet with HR and compliance about the changes we want to get their buy-in. So, let me know what you think so we can set up a time to talk about this plan.

Best,

Sigmund

Will Michael live long enough to care about Sigmund's endless unfocused request? No. Read the following revision that has been sprayed with editorial Windex.

Revision—without the unneeded details (66 words)

Michael,

Now that I'm back from vacation, I'd like to propose some next steps for changing the RFP language database:

1. Meet with the four department heads to come to a consensus about which sections we should change first

2. Meet with HR and compliance to get their buy-in.

So, can you please let me know when you and I can meet to get this ball rolling?

Best,

Sigmund

4. Write with intelligence and political awareness

Intelligence manifests itself differently in corporate America compared to its displays in academia or in your personal life. For instance, when you IM or text, you display one kind of intelligence about what is appropriate. In college, when you wrote academic papers, you probably paved the road to intelligence with words like "hegemonic museumification" and *au contraire*—but *au contraire* in business? A big mistake. In business, you must chart a course between the excessive formality of academia and the abbreviated staccato of Twitter and instant messaging.

Keep your diction simple and direct

Abandon the academic vocabulary your parents paid so much for you to acquire; instead, let your speech guide you and choose the simpler word. Although prying your fingers off your academic vocabulary may cause you actual physical pain, the benefits will be huge, since you will never ever have to interpret anything like this again:

Example—academic writing that complicates an idea that wasn't even obvious to begin with

> Such authority seems singularly unstable, complicated by the perpetual *fort/da,* wherein art violates the very boundaries it asserts, by the fact that some negation of the negation can always allow the passé an apparent return, by the fact that the art system—the institution named Art—aggressively stabilizes its perpetuity through all kinds of de-stabilizing processes.[1]

Yes, and we hope to complicate your perpetual *fort/da* with our intermittent *quid pro quos.*

Adopt the necessary formality and extend the generous courtesies that the corporate culture requires—and do so with humility

You are not writing to your friends, or even your supporters, necessarily; you are writing to people who spend their days eyeball to eyeball with alligators, and you will serve them well and secure your place in their hearts if you:

- **Take responsibility and keep the initiative.** Don't ask senior managers to get back to you about your interest in doing a rotation in their area or to hear your suggestions about how the firm could be managed better. If you want a rotation, explain how you can be an asset to the division and keep the initiative: tell the manager you'll follow up. If you think you know how to manage the firm better, prove it first in your day-to-day success.

- **Avoid the abbreviations and slang** that populate instant messaging and texting because no one is going to LOL.

Consider the following misunderstanding of how overconfidence operates in business:

Original—overconfident and fails to extend the proper courtesies

> Hi Colin,
>
> I am Simon Davis and I am currently working as an intern with Mark Scofield in R & D. I will be applying for a rotation and I have some questions to ensure that I receive an assignment that works well for me.
>
> In my last rotation, the person I reported to knew less than I did and, in my opinion, handled issues badly.
>
> I am hoping we can meet next Wednesday after 3 p.m., so please call me as soon as possible at the number below.

Just a hunch, but we're guessing this meeting never happened, and that Simon just went driving by in an ice-cream truck wearing a clown hat. Here's the right approach, which marries confidence and courtesy:

Revision—extends the proper courtesies

> Dear Colin,
>
> As an intern in R & D with Mark Scofield, I am writing to ask if you would be willing to meet with me to discuss whether my skills might be a good match for your division. Mark suggested that I contact you, as he mentioned that you need someone knowledge-able about regression analysis and quantitative analysis—both skills I have.
>
> I will call your office in the next few days to follow up, and hope that you can find time in your busy schedule for a short meeting.

If not, perhaps you can direct me to someone else? If you have any questions in the meantime, my phone number is 123.456.7890, and my email is simondavis@wahoo.com.

Thank you for considering my request.

Best,

You can build a brilliant career with words. Use these strategies to construct effective documents built upon your understanding and insight. If you do, you'll know success for sure, and we hope you'll hire us when you're running the firm.

CHAPTER 22

If you want to make sure your writing is right

You write to prompt understanding and action, so evaluate every decision you make as writer in light of this goal. Always write to help clients—both internal and external—feel informed and confident of their decisions. **Become your reader!**

Use the pointers in this section as a quick checklist to make sure your writing is right.

1. Organization

- **Organize from most-to-least important information** most of the time. Avoid writing academically and building to your conclusions.

- **Be sure your opening sentences pass the "So what?" test,** and highlight the relevance of your message or clearly identify its value. Apply this test to all documents and email, so readers know immediately why they should keep reading.

- **Be sure each topic sentence presents a main or key point.** Reread all of your topic sentences to make sure they create an outline of your key points.

2. Content

- **Evaluate every detail you want to include:** always ask, "Will this detail help improve the quality of my readers' understanding or improve the quality of the decision that needs to be made?" If not, omit it.

- **Provide judgments, not just details.** You get paid to make judgments, so be sure to do so. Never soak your readers with a fire hose of detail and forget to tell them why they are getting wet.

3. Visual Arrangement

Use visual strategies to help readers see your key points in all of your documents, even in your email. Make judicious use of:

- **Headings and subheadings** to identify key categories of information.

- **Boldface and italics** to highlight critical points you don't want readers to miss.

- **Bullets and numbering** to pull out important lists and actions. Don't use bullets for points that don't deserve the added emphasis, and don't use bullets like confetti to mark every point.

- **Tables and charts** to convey technical or numerical information. Introduce tables and diagrams with sentences that capture value, not just superficial descriptions.

- **Short paragraphs.** If a paragraph is long enough to wear as a dress, it's too long. About seven to nine lines is a good average length.

4. Style

- **Let your speech guide you and keep it simple.** If you could not read aloud what you've written to a reader face to face without feeling as though it were actually authored by Skippy, your evil twin, rewrite it. Put the action in the verb, use the active voice, use the small word, and edit out empty words.

- **Keep your sentence length average between 15 and 28 words,** depending on the document. Just because you know how to write a 76-word sentence doesn't mean you should.

- **Remember that an overattachment to your own style is a waste of time.**

- **Proofread.** Proofread for minor errors in spelling and punctuation, which can diminish your credibility.

As you meet the challenges that press against the gates of every business day—have no fear. Even when these challenges appear more terrifying than the Visigoths, just use our strategies, and you're sure to know victory.

Endnotes

Chapter 3

1. Kathy Werlein, an editor in the Research Division at R.W. Baird in Milwaukee, suggests this general rule: "If you have more than four punctuation marks in a single sentence, it may be overly complicated, so be careful." Although we have been known to violate this rule, we do so only under the influence of Pinot Noir, and we are professionals: do not try this at home. Interview with Kathy Werlein (July 22, 2009).

Chapter 4

1. In technical and financial documents, such as credit requests, confidential memos of information, and white papers, you will use fewer pronouns, simply given the conventions that define these documents. Still, always let your speech guide your choices on the page, so that you don't complicate a complex message with complex language and structures. See also chapter 1: If you want to write persuasively; chapter 2: If you want readers to actually read and respond to what you've written; chapter 3: If you want to write clearly and concisely.

Chapter 13

1. Renae Merle, "Boeing CEO Resigns Over Affair with Subordinate," *Washington Post*, March 8, 2005, p. A01.

2. Wendy Tanaka, "Microsoft 'Caves' to Intel," *Forbes.com*, February 28, 2008, www.forbes.com/2008/02/28/ microsoft-vista-intel-tech-ebiz-cx_wt_0228vista.html (accessed August 15, 2009).

3.	Tom Krazit, "Microsft E-Mails Reveal Intel Pressure Over Vista," CNET.com, February 28, 2008, news.cnet.com/ 8301-13579_3-9882376-37.html?tag=mncol (accessed August 15, 2009).

4.	Tamar Lewin, "Chevron Settles Sexual Harassment Charges," *New York Times*, February 22, 1995, www.nytimes .com/1995/02/22/us/chevron-settles-sexual-harassment-charges.html (accessed August 15, 2009).

5.	Alicia Mundy, *Dispensing with the Truth: The Victims, the Drug Companies, and the Dramatic Story Behind the Battle over Phen-Fen* (New York: St. Martin's Griffin, 2001), 200.

6.	David Teather, "Star US Banker Faces Jail after Guilty Verdict," *The Guardian*, May 4, 2004, www.guardian.co.uk/technology/ 2004/may/04/business.usnews (accessed August 15, 2009).

7.	Jessica Guynn, "Quattrone Dealing with a Comeback," *San Francisco Chronicle*, January 25, 2007, www.sfgate.com/cgi-bin/ article.cgi?f=/c/a/2007/01/25/ (accessed August 15, 2009).

Chapter 14

1.	Lindsey Tanner, "Apology a Tool to Avoid Malpractice Suits," *The Boston Globe*, November 12, 2004, www.boston.com/news/ nation/articles/2004/11/12/apology_a_tool_to_avoid_ malpractice_suits/ (accessed September 8, 2009).

	The hospitals in the University of Michigan Health System have been encouraging doctors since 2002 to apologize for mistakes. The system's annual attorney fees have since dropped from $3 million to $1 million, and malpractice lawsuits and notices of intent to sue have fallen from 262 filed in 2001 to about 130 per year.

2.	Rita Marie Barsella, "Sincere Apologies Are Priceless," *Nurse.com*, July 16, 2007, news.nurse.com/apps/pbcs.dll/ article?AID=2007307090023 (accessed September 8, 2009).

	Lucian L. Leape, MD, one of the founders of the National Patient Safety Foundation and author of the 1994 *Journal of the American Medical Association* article "Error in Medicine," advocates full

Endnotes 205

disclosure as a means of preserving the trust he calls the "cornerstone" of the relationship between the patient and practitioner. He says an apology starts the healing process for both patient and the practitioner.

Chapter 16

1. For deep and detailed information about PowerPoint, see Cliff Atkinson, *Beyond Bullet Points: Using Microsoft® Office Power-Point® 2007 to Create Presentations That Inform, Motivate, and Inspire*; (Sebastopol, CA: O'Reilly Media, 2007); for technical information about keystrokes, refer to Doug Lowe's *PowerPoint 2007 for Dummies* (Hoboken, NJ: John Wiley & Sons, 2007).

2. Michael Alley, *The Craft of Scientific Presentations*, 2nd ed. (New York: Springer-Verlag, 2010).

Chapter 19

1. Interview with Sam Biardo (September 5, 2009).

Chapter 20

1. Max Ehrmann, *Desiderata: A Poem for a Way of Life* (New York: Crown, 1999), 10.

2. Ibid.

Chapter 21

1. Bill Brown, "Counting (Art and Discipline)," *Critical Inquiry* 35.4 (Summer 2009): 1035.

Acknowledgments

David Zehren, of Zehren-Friedman Associates, made this book possible nearly thirty years ago when he did not equate inexperience and fashion ineptitude with incompetence. His life has been a gesture of generosity and optimism: a visionary, he sees potential where others do not, and for that, we are grateful beyond words.

Early on, three senior executives at the former First National Bank of Chicago and the Northern Trust Company recognized that our passion for clear writing could help us do good and do well. Scott Bates stands alone as an inspiration to anyone fortunate enough to work with him; he believed in us and his belief inspired courage, especially when we were just learning how to navigate the corporate landscape. Fred Stewart, a model of humility and intelligence, offered us his support, good will, and insight over many years. John Ballantine helped us understand a critical approach to good organization that we still teach today— even though we doubt he remembers us.

We are grateful to everyone at Stonesong Press, but offer our special thanks to Katie Feiereisel. This book would never have seen the light of day had she not seen its value. She worked tirelessly to help us bring this book to life, and if it were up to us, we'd make her Queen.

Our thanks as well to Veronica Randall, our editor at Ten Speed Press: she countered every anxiety and each misstep with wit and patience. Chloe Rawlins, also at Ten Speed, bore our endless requests for changes without complaint or recrimination.

We also thank Mary Biardo, at Technology Advisors, Inc., for being ever available and responsive to our questions about office protocols and customer relationship management software.

We thank our clients and all those who have attended our writing seminars over the past nearly thirty years. You gave our professional lives meaning, and inspired us with your commitment to harnessing the power of language. We even thank those of you who behaved as though you were insufficiently loved as children; even you helped us learn and grow. Still, most of you were too good to us: your intelligence, your open-mindedness, and your humor have left lasting imprints on our hearts.

Our children, Katie, Annie, and Dave Berndtson, and Fraser Brown, are the heart of the inspiration that has defined our life's work and helped produce this book. Years ago, one of us was undone by a ravenous maternal appetite, and the other by a visceral hatred of cubicles and fluorescent lights, so we quit our day jobs and began crafting our careers during naps and nights. Our love for our children has illuminated every step of the way to this very page.

We also thank our husbands: Bill Brown was always willing to arbitrate especially arcane grammatical points and enthusiastically offered up his academic writing to serve as the antithesis of business writing. Keith Berndtson was a rock star of support and did his best to stay out of the way as the book took shape. We both hope to stay married for a long time to come, but we guess that may depend on how the book sales go.

Finally, we give a nod to each other. With each other, we have seen glimpses of our best selves and our worst, but always through a lens of love and respect.

Index

Product liability issues, 114

Pronouns

in academic writing, 164

eliminating repetition with, 55–56

importance of, 163

strengthening connection with
readers, 53–56, 94

Proofreading, 61, 135, 183, 203

Proposals

designed for quick reading, 168

highlighting the value of, 149–56

proposal writer software for, 148

sentence length for, 49

Public companies, 119

Punctuation, 32–33, 41, 85, 203

Q

Qualifications, presenting without
pretense, 10–11

R

Reader, becoming your, 70, 201

Relevant versus irrelevant content

distinguishing between, 7–10, 82

evaluating, 202

in financial documents, 128–30

in PowerPoint presentations, 137–39

Re: lines, 14–15

Repetition

bullets eliminating, 31–32

editing out, 130, 135

excessive, 43

pronouns eliminating, 55–56

Representing yourself well, 174–75

Responsibility, taking, 198

Resumes

accomplishments section, 178–81

defining your experience, 183

gaps in, 183

inserting key words, 182

matching potential employer's
requirements, 177–78

organizing details in order of
relevance, 181

overview, 176

page length, 182

proofreading, 183

statement of objective, 177–78

templates for, 181

visual aspects of, 182

years of career and experiences, 182

RET (Request, Explanation or Details,
Thanks) template, 76–78

S

Sales documents/letters

adapting from well-written letters,
166–68

client-targeted benefits in, 156–60

competitively persuasive, 148

designed for quick reading, 168

effective versus ineffective, 161–62

Executive Summary, 81, 149–56

speech as guide for writing, 162–66

templates for, 166–68

using language that connects with
clients, 160–66

Salutations and closings, 84

Senior management, writing for

asking for guidance from, 82

distinguishing relevant versus
irrelevant content, 82

feedback for, 83, 85

handling differences of opinion, 85

headings for, 20

information organized from most-to-
least important, 81, 122–25

overview, 80

paragraph length for, 83

preferences and concerns of
management, 84–85

reviewing examples of similar
documents, 82–83

writing styles to avoid, 83–84

Sentence length

average, 49–50, 203

for emails, letters, memos, and
updates, 49

for financial documents, 131–32

long and convoluted, 41

for reports, credit analyses,
proposals, 49

for writing that flows, 62